Praise for *It's a Sweet World*

"I have had black and white cookies everywhere in the country. Bea's Bakery is by far the best I've had for the last forty-five years. Same recipe, same deliciousness, the very best way to celebrate a cookie day, the beginning of the day, the best way to celebrate any day."

—Henry Winkler, author of *Being Henry: The Fonz…and Beyond*

"Whenever I see a Bea's Bakery box, a wave of excitement washes over me. Inside is the promise of the best dessert, ready to turn any moment into a celebration."

—Missy Birns, head of talent development and casting at Warner Bros. Discovery

"Bea's Bakery's Ube Challah always reminds me of the pound cake from my home country, Zimbabwe. Every bite of the soft and sweet treat brings back fond memories."

—Tongayi Chirisa, actor behind Cheetor in *Transformers: Rise of the Beast*

"There is no other bakery in the world that can match Bea's Bakery's mouthwatering rainbow cookies. The marzipan flavor is undeniable in every bite."

—Steven Paul, chairman and CEO of Crystal Sky Pictures

"My kids and I love Bea's chocolate rugelach. We always make it a point to stop at Bea's Bakery where Lenny and Adaeze bake the best sweets in Los Angeles."

—Tom Arnold, comedian and actor behind Arnie Thomas on *Roseanne*

"I had the great pleasure of working with Lenny and Adaeze on an episode of *Mystery Diners* several years ago. And we have been friends ever since. As an entrepreneur myself, I have always been amazed at not only Lenny's level of business skills and integrity, but also his deep commitment to always producing the highest quality and freshest products in the industry. When it comes to restaurants and bakeries, Lenny knows his stuff. He's smart, articulate, and has a talent for creating baked goods that people love so much, they keep coming back for more."

—Charles Stiles, host of Food Network's *Mystery Diners* and president of Mystery Shopper Services

"Hands down, the rugelach at Bea's Bakery is my favorite. There is always a surprise flavor in the filling—be it nuts, chocolate or fruit. Whatever the variety, I will eat Bea's rugelach any day of the week."

—Brad Pomerance, host & executive vice president of Jewish Life TV

It's a Sweet
WORLD

It's a Sweet WORLD

Recipes from Around the Globe at Bea's Bakery

LENNY ROSENBERG
and ADAEZE NWANONYIRI

Owners of Bea's Bakery, one of the last full-service homemade Jewish-style bakeries in Los Angeles

MIAMI

Copyright © 2025 by Lenny Rosenberg and Adaeze Nwanonyiri.
Published by Mango Publishing Group, a division of Mango Media Inc.

Cover Design: Carmen Fortunato
Cover Photo: Willy SanJuan Photography
Layout & Design: Carmen Fortunato
Interior Photos: Willy SanJuan Photography

Mango is an active supporter of authors' rights to free speech and artistic expression in their books. The purpose of copyright is to encourage authors to produce exceptional works that enrich our culture and our open society.

Uploading or distributing photos, scans or any content from this book without prior permission is theft of the author's intellectual property. Please honor the author's work as you would your own. Thank you in advance for respecting our author's rights.

For permission requests, please contact the publisher at:
Mango Publishing Group
5966 South Dixie Highway, Suite 300
Miami, FL 33143

For special orders, quantity sales, course adoptions and corporate sales, please email the publisher at sales@mango.bz. For trade and wholesale sales, please contact Ingram Publisher Services at customer.service@ingramcontent.com or +1.800.509.4887.

It's a Sweet World: Recipes from Around the Globe at Bea's Bakery

Printed in the United States of America

ISBNs: (p) 978-1-6-8481774-0 (e) 978-1-6-8481775-7

BISAC: CKB045000, COOKING / Regional & Cultural / International

LCCN: 2024949474

Table of Contents

Preface 10

Foreword 12

Introduction: History of Bea's Bakery and a Tribute to Original Owners 14

CHAPTER 1: BREADS 17

    Traditional Challah with Variations (Jewish) 19

    Ube Challah (Filipino) 23

    Sour Cream Chocolate Chip Loaf (American) 27

CHAPTER 2: CAKES AND BARS 31

    Sour Cream Cheesecake (Greek) 33

    Poppy Seed Roll (Ukrainian) 37

    Honey Cake with Variations (Ancient and Global) 41

    Nigerian Pound Cake (Nigerian) 45

    Napoleons (French) 49

    Hungarian Seven-Layer Cake (Hungarian) 55

    Yum Yum Cakes (Southern) 61

    Red Velvet Kola Nut Cupcakes (Nigerian) 65

    Lamington Coconut Bars (Australian) 69

    Lemon Bars (American) 73

    Nigerian Coconut Candy Bars (Nigerian) 77

    Pecan Bars (Southern) 81

    Flourless Chocolate Cake (Italian) 85

CHAPTER 3: COOKIES 89

- Ube Cookies (Filipino) 91
- Chinese Cookies (Jewish / Chinese) 95
- Rainbow Cookies (Italian American) 99
- Butter Cookies (Danish) 103
- Mexican Wedding Cookies/Snowballs (Mexican / Ukrainian) 107
- Triple Chocolate Cookies (American) 111
- Spritz Cookies (German) 115
- Chocolate Rugelach (Polish / Jewish) 119
- Sugar-Free Cinnamon Raisin Rugelach (Jewish) 123
- Nigerian Ground Nut Cookies (Nigerian) 127
- Almond Horn (Danish) 131
- Black and White Cookies (American) 135
- Green & Whites (Nigerian) 139
- Oatmeal Raisin Cookies (American) 143
- Mandelbrot (Jewish) 147
- Coconut Macaroon (Italian/Jewish) 151
- French Rolled Florentine (French) 155
- Italian Cannoli (Italian) 159
- Gingerbread Cookies (Egyptian) 163
- Almond Macaroon Cookies (Italian) 167

CHAPTER 4: PIES AND PUDDINGS 171

- Fresh Fruit Tarte (French) 173
- Bea's Classic Pumpkin Pie (American) 177
- Lemon Meringue Pie (American) 181
- Adaeze's Southern Sweet Potato Pie (Southern) 185
- Lenny's Famous New York Apple Pie (American / English) 189
- Chocolate Mousse Pudding (French) 193
- English Bread Pudding (English) 197

CHAPTER 5: MUFFINS AND SCONES ... 201

- New England Bran Muffin (American) ... 203
- Blueberry Muffins (American) ... 207
- Double Chocolate Muffin (American) ... 211
- Kichel—with a Sugar-Free Version (Jewish) ... 215
- British Buttermilk Scones (English) ... 219
- Oat Currant Scones (Scottish) ... 223

CHAPTER 6: SPECIALTY SWEET BREADS ... 227

- Chocolate Babka (Polish) ... 229
- Irish Soda Bread (Irish) ... 233
- Nigerian Cornbread (Nigerian) ... 237

CHAPTER 7: MORE SWEET TREATS ... 241

- Apple Noodle Kugel (Jewish) ... 243
- Matzo Kugel (German / Jewish) ... 247
- Nigerian Egg Rolls (Nigerian) ... 251
- Éclair (French) ... 255
- Danish Pastries (Danish) ... 261
- Butter Streusel (German) ... 265
- Brownies (American) ... 269
- Rum Balls (Danish) ... 273

Acknowledgements ... 276

About the Authors ... 278

Preface

Years ago, my husband and I bought two beloved, family-run restaurants in Los Angeles: Nate 'n Al's delicatessen in Beverly Hills and The Apple Pan in Westwood. Both were regarded as institutions. They had been around for decades, but, more importantly, they were places where we had eaten while growing up and then shared with our children and grandchildren. The memories were as special as the food. My husband and I feel it is important to maintain the fabric of our childhoods, those special places that helped make us who we are so that we can pass that on to future generations, and so, in that spirit, when these two restaurants fell on hard times and were about to shut their doors, we stepped in and kept them going.

Our friends Lenny Rosenberg and Adaeze Nwanonyiri did that same thing with Bea's Bakery in Tarzana. Bea's is one of those special places for me. I grew up in the San Fernando Valley, and my mother would take me and my brother and sister there when she wanted to pick up fresh cookies or bread to have in the house. It was the same for countless families like ours. Bea's first opened its doors in 1968. It was a family-run traditional Jewish bakery. I remember walking in with my mother and experiencing the thrill of the display case full of challah and rye bread, pastries and cakes, and cookies—rugelach, mandel bread, Black and Whites, and brownies. My favorites were the éclairs and the coconut bars. The éclairs had real custard filling, and I still get the coconut bars and serve them for dessert.

That's the tradition I'm talking about. I have taken my own children and grandchildren to Bea's, and now my favorite memories are of them having their own memories of walking into Bea's and getting excited about picking out their favorite treats. I was thrilled when Lenny and Adaeze purchased Bea's from the son of its original owners and committed to preserving its wonderful traditions and memories, just as my husband and I had done with Nate 'n Al's and The Apple Pan. Not only have they done that, but Adaeze has drawn on her own multicultural background to give Bea's a contemporary refresh. Yes, it's still a traditional Jewish bakery, but the display case also boasts pandan coconut crinkle cookies, Vietnamese coffee-stuffed cookies, and Adaeze's Nigerian-inspired red velvet kola nut cupcakes. As Adaeze likes to say, there's a sweet at this table for everyone.

I applaud Lenny and Adaeze. I believe it's important to save the old recipes and traditions we grew up with and pass them on to our children and grandchildren. And that is what you will find in this wonderful book. *It's a Sweet World: Recipes from Around the Globe at Bea's Bakery* is a collection of everyday and special occasion recipes that will let you create new memories and continue to indulge in those we all remember and love.

Based on my own experiences, I will tell you that life is best with a sweet and this book is full of them. Enjoy.

—Shelli Azoff

Foreword

With this marvelous cookbook, you are being treated to a tremendous gift: the best of Jewish baking. This is a subject I know more about than perhaps almost anyone. I have been in the delicatessen business for forty-five years. I'm third generation; in 1927, my grandfather opened the Rialto, the first Jewish deli on Broadway in New York City. I knew how to make pastrami before I was bar mitzvahed. I have run delis in New York, Los Angeles, and Houston, where I have been for the past twenty-five years, and where, as I have frequently said, "I have the privilege of showing how life without a great deli is really no life at all."

What makes a great deli? Naturally it's the food. But it's also the life that happens within it, the cast of characters who make it a home away from home. My deli, Kenny & Ziggy's, is at the center of the Jewish community. We do all the events—births, brises, naming ceremonies, bar mitzvahs, sweet sixteen parties, weddings, and shiva. More than just food, a great deli is about family and tradition. There's nothing like getting a tap on the shoulder from a big, tall guy who I remember coming in as a little kid—and he's still got a cookie in his hand.

So believe me when I tell you that Bea's Bakery is one of those special places that is more than you initially see. When you step into Bea's Bakery, you step into another world—a world dating back to the 1960s and full of all the stuff you grew up with as a kid, the stuff most bakeries don't make anymore or even know how to make. It's a bakery that has great rye and pumpernickel bread and challah, plus all the great Jewish butter cookies, rugelach, hamantaschen, babka, and Danish. It's also a bakery where grandmas brought their grandchildren and now those grandchildren are bringing their own children and grandchildren. As we say in Hebrew, *l'dor v'dor*, or generation to generation.

This is what has made Bea's a Los Angeles institution for almost sixty years, and it's what my friend Lenny Rosenberg and his wife Adaeze have continued since purchasing Bea's from the founder's son, Jules Litwak. I'm the matchmaker who heard that Julius wanted to retire but couldn't find anyone to take over Bea's. I immediately thought of Lenny. He's one of a kind, and Bea's is the last of its kind—in other words, a perfect match. They made a deal, and Julius passed away two weeks later.

As we say in Yiddish, Bea's has got *gantse megile,* or the whole thing, and with this marvelous cookbook, the best of Bea's is available to everyone, especially those who live too far to drive to Tarzana. Rejoice, celebrate, and bake! The recipes you'll find on the following pages might seem like they are for cookies and coffee cakes and other delicious things, but they are really recipes for hugs and kisses and smiles and expressions of love that make me happy there's a Bea's in this world.

—Ziggy Gruber

Introduction

History of Bea's Bakery and a Tribute to Original Owners

Bring the Baked Goodness of Bea's into Your Home

Bea's Bakery has been a much-loved fixture of California life for almost sixty years, providing comfort and nourishment to thousands in what was once a rich tradition of Jewish bakeries in America. Originally opened in 1968 by Sol Litwak and his son Jules, it was named after Sol's wife Beatrice, known affectionately as "Bea," and run by the father and son for over fifty years.

After Sol and Bea passed away, their son took over the iconic family bakery in Tarzana, Los Angeles, and continued working there until his death in 2023 at the age of eighty-seven. The previous year, Jules had decided it was time to pass the family business on to the next generation. He had many offers but knew that selling it to dynamic husband and wife Lenny Rosenberg and Adaeze Nwanonyiri, was *bashert*—a Yiddish word for something that's meant to be.

When Lenny, the son of a Hungarian baker who'd survived the Holocaust, married Adaeze, a Nigerian designer from a noble African tribe, it was a marriage made in heaven. With their joint experience, multicultural background, and a strong desire to bring everyone to the table, the couple became co-owners of LARS Restaurants, the parent company of Bea's Bakery, with a business model to reimagine and redesign favorite old restaurants and breathe new life into them.

As hosts of *It's a Sweet World* for Jewish Life Television, they also knew the power of food to bring people together and transport them back to the traditional tastes and aromas of their childhoods, while bringing them up to date with healthy options that cater to all.

This, their first book, is a celebration of the best recipes from Bea's, including Jewish and Nigerian signature dishes, along with scores of tasty treats from around the globe that will appeal to people of all nations and creeds. Theirs is food for the soul, and each recipe includes a short history and associated memory, as well as a photo and suggestions for the best occasions to enjoy it, whether it's a wedding, a baby shower, or just a family get-together. If you love to bake—and enjoy discovering new favorites as well as timeless old standards—you'll find yourself making the recipes again and again to enjoy in the comfort of your own home.

CHAPTER 1

Breads

Traditional Challah with Variations
(Jewish)

You don't have to be Jewish to love the eggy, buttery delight that is challah bread. Few loaves match up to its appearance, texture, or taste. The name comes from the Hebrew for "portion" when God is said to have commanded Moses and the Israelites to set aside a portion (or "challah") of their bread for local Jewish priests in thanks for ending their exile and entering the Holy Land.

Breaking bread is a traditional ritual in most world religions, bringing friends and families together. But few hold the bread itself in such high regard as Jews do, who carry the braided challah to the candlelit Shabbat table like an offering at sunset and place it center stage. It is a metaphorical representation of the "manna from heaven" that fell on a Friday to keep people going through the Sabbath. As blessings are made and wine is sipped, the soft, flavorsome bread that most closely resembles brioche is pulled apart and shared.

The traditional braided loaf is the most common variation for Shabbat, as three strands of dough are plaited together to form twelve mounds, said to represent the ceremonial loaves kept for the twelve tribes of Israel on the altar of the Holy Temple of Jerusalem. At Rosh Hashanah, the Jewish New Year, the bread is molded into a round shape to represent completeness.

By taking something as physical as a loaf of bread and elevating it to the spiritual, the Jewish tradition instills blessings and good thoughts into those gathered around the table, as well as providing them with good, wholesome nourishment. And the beauty of challah bread is that you can make all manner of variations, including the ones listed below: apple and honey, chocolate chip, seeded, and raisin.

Better still, if there are any leftovers after Friday night dinner, it makes the perfect French toast the following morning. Mazel tov!

INGREDIENTS:

DOUGH:
- Fresh yeast—1¾ teaspoons (4 g)
- Vegetable oil—¼ cup (60 mL)
- Whole large eggs—2½ (113 mL)
- Salt—½ Tablespoon (10 g)
- Honey—¼ cup (60 mL)
- All-purpose flour—4½ cups (540 g)
- Sliced fresh apple—½ cup (55 g)

TOPPING:
- Egg yolks—2 (30mL)
- Water—1 teaspoon (5 mL)

INSTRUCTIONS:

1. Pour fresh yeast, oil, and eggs into a mixing bowl and mix by hand till the fresh yeast is fully incorporated.
2. Add the remaining dough ingredients into the mixing bowl.
3. Mix at second speed for 10 minutes till the dough separates from the bowl and is slightly warm to the touch.
4. Separate the dough into 18-oz. (510 g) pieces.
5. Cut each 18-oz. piece into six pieces and braid or roll into round challah.
6. Cover with plastic and store somewhere warm for 45 minutes or until the loaf is 50 percent larger.
7. Beat the egg yolks and add the water. Brush the egg wash over the challah before you put it in the oven.
8. Bake for 45 minutes at 325°F (170°C).

Yields two 1 lb. 2 oz. (1008 g) challahs

Traditional Challah with Chocolate Chip, Raisins or Seeds

Follow the challah recipe on the previous page with the following differences:

1. Substitute granulated sugar for honey.
2. Eliminate the fresh sliced apples.
3. Add any one of these ingredients in step 2:

   - Chocolate chips—¾ cup (227 g)
   - Raisins—¾ cup (119 g)
   - Poppy seeds—½ cup (130 g)
   - Sesame seeds—½ cup (130 g)

4. Save a small handful of the chocolate chips, raisins, or seeds to sprinkle on top after you wash the bread and before baking.

Enjoy Challah for Friday night blessings, special occasions, and anytime.

Ube Challah
(Filipino)

Friday night dinners when I was growing up in Plainview, Long Island, were sacrosanct in our household. The youngest of five children, I would wait for my father, Bob, to return home an hour before sundown—the only night he did—carrying two braided challah bread loaves from his bakery, made by hand from his mother's recipe.

As was traditional in Jewish homes around the world, my mother Clara would light the candles in the silver candlesticks and make the blessing, and then my father would take a knife and, peeling back the embroidered cloth that always covered the loaves, cut into the fresh, eggy bread. Along with my sister and my three brothers, I looked forward to the one night of the week where we ate together as a family, as my father wouldn't normally leave his busy Peter Pan bakery.

A survivor of the Holocaust as a teenager, he never spoke of his time in Auschwitz or the loss of most of his family, and he rarely showed emotion. But after years in a place where he survived on bread, even though it was such poor quality, he never lost his love for rye. I knew nothing of his past as a child, but I did know how important it was for him to come home for Shabbat and break bread with the family he was nearly denied.

Challah was always on the menu at his many bakeries, and it is still a bestseller at Bea's Bakery, where we decided to give it a unique, multicultural twist by merging the Jewish tradition with a Filipino staple—ube. By incorporating these fresh purple yams that are shipped to us from Manila, the inside of the challah turns a delightful lilac hue and has a distinctively sweet taste. Just as my family's celebrations wouldn't have been complete without challah bread, no holiday in the Philippines would be the same without this delicious treat. Now our customers from all corners of the globe get to enjoy it too.

Lenny

INGREDIENTS:

DOUGH:
- Dry active fresh yeast—1½ Tablespoons (29 g)
- Granulated sugar—¾ cup (152 g)
- Lukewarm water—1¼ cups (300 mL)
- Vegetable oil—¼ cup (60 mL)
- Large eggs—2 (90 mL)
- Ube extract—2 teaspoons (14 g)
- Unbleached bread flour—4½ cups (571 g)
- Sea salt—½ teaspoon (3 g)
- Dehydrated ube powder (buy from your local market)—4 oz. (112 g)

TOPPING:
- Egg yolks—2 (30 mL)
- Water—1 teaspoon (5 mL)

INSTRUCTIONS:

Dough:
1. Place fresh yeast, ½ teaspoon sugar, and lukewarm water in a large mixing bowl. Stir and allow to bloom for 5 minutes.
2. Add the remaining sugar, oil, eggs, and ube extract, and mix until incorporated.
3. Add the flour, salt, and ube powder to the mixture. Knead using the dough hook attachment of your mixer for about 10 minutes, until the dough is smooth and elastic.

4. Place dough in a greased bowl and cover with a damp towel. Allow to rise for about 2 hours.
5. Divide the dough into two. Then divide each challah into three long strands. Braid the challahs and form into your desired shape.
6. Place challahs on a baking pan, lined with parchment paper. Allow the dough to rise (proof) for another 45 minutes.
7. Preheat the oven to 375°F (190°C) while proofing.
8. Beat the egg yolks and add the water. Brush the egg wash over the challah before you put it in the oven.
9. Bake for 25 to 30 minutes.

Yields two 1 lb. 2 oz. (1008 g) loaves

Enjoy Ube Challah for holidays, special occasions, and anytime.

Sour Cream Chocolate Chip Loaf (American)

What could be more American than chocolate chip anything? It's certainly always been a favorite at Bea's. But did you know that chocolate chip cookies were reportedly created by chef and food author Ruth Graves Wakefield in her famous Massachusetts Toll House Inn almost ninety years ago, when she decided to add a few chunks from a sweet chocolate bar to her cookie dough?

Her cookies became so popular that she struck a deal with the chocolate bar company to use her recipe on its wrapping in exchange for a lifetime supply of the cooking chocolate they went on to develop at her suggestion. Go, Ruth!

Lenny's father loved this chocolate chip loaf so much that he made it in every bakery he owned, going right back to the Walls Bakery in Hewett, Long Island, forty years ago. This delicious, no-fuss recipe that takes approximately an hour to make is loaded with Ruth-inspired chunky chocolate chips and the magical ingredient of sour cream to add moisture, taste, and texture. Sour cream is just regular cream that's been thickened and soured to give it a creamy consistency, tender airiness, and distinctively tangy taste, like Greek yogurt. Its high fat content also gives a unique richness to any cake, along with the eggs that bind the mixture.

Add a dash of vanilla essence for summer freshness and dust it with powdered sugar, and you have a winning treat that will gladden any heart, 365 days of the year. This is a melt-in-your-mouth loaf that probably won't last long once it's out of the oven. They certainly sell like hot cakes at Bea's!

INGREDIENTS:

- Cake flour—12 oz. (336 g)
- All-purpose shortening—8 oz. (224 g)
- Granulated sugar—8 oz. (224 g)
- Table salt—1 pinch
- Baking soda—⅛ oz. (4 g)
- Vanilla—1 small splash
- Whole large eggs—3 (135 mL)
- Sour cream—8 oz. (224 mL)
- Dark chocolate chips—12 oz. (340 g)

INSTRUCTIONS:

1. Pour all ingredients into a mixing bowl.
2. Mix at second speed for 4 to 5 minutes or until the mix is smooth.
3. Spray three 12-oz. loaf pans with baking spray.
4. Pour the batter into the prepared loaf pans.
5. Bake at 325°F (170°C) for 50 minutes.

Yields three 1 lb. 2 oz. (1,512 g) loaves

CHAPTER 2

Cakes and Bars

Sour Cream Cheesecake
(Greek)

We often think of cheesecake as being an all-American dessert that's maybe a couple of hundred years old, but both those assumptions couldn't be further from the truth. It will probably surprise you to know that cheesecake was served to athletes during the first ever Olympic Games in Greece in 776 BC—that's four thousand years ago!

It was also used as a traditional wedding cake, using a simple recipe of pounded curd cheese baked with honey and flour on an earthenware griddle, and lauded as a quick source of protein and energy. The original recipe has been adapted and modernized multiple times over the centuries, and it was the Romans who took it back to Italy after they invaded Greece, adding eggs and cooking it under hot bricks. As the Roman Empire expanded, this beloved recipe traveled with them and was given its own unique variations by early Europeans who gave it a pastry base or crust, adding sugar, fruit, spices, and milk, depending on what was in season.

The first English cheesecake recipes appeared in the fourteenth century, and the popular dessert soon transferred to the colonies—including America in the 1700s—where chefs added more delicate ingredients like lemon, vanilla, and rosewater. It wasn't until the invention of cream cheese in New York in 1870 that curd cheese was phased out and the kind of recipe we know and love today came into fashion, becoming richer and creamier still.

The cheesecake we make at Bea's is another firm favorite and gets its velvety texture from three and a half pounds of cream cheese, a cup of sour cream, and some whole milk. Topped with mashed strawberries, chocolate swirl, or a berry mix, there's enough energy and protein there even for an Olympian.

INGREDIENTS:

- Cream cheese—3½ cups (765 g)
- Granulated sugar—1¼ cups (250 g)
- Whole large eggs—3 (135 mL)
- Whole milk—1 cup (240 mL)
- Sour cream—½ cup (117 g)
- Finely crushed graham crackers—½ cup (13 g)
- Melted unsalted butter—¼ cup (55 g)

INSTRUCTIONS:

1. Pour cream cheese and sugar into a bowl and mix at first speed for 2 minutes till smooth.
2. Add eggs, milk, and sour cream into the bowl and mix again for 2 minutes or until smooth.
3. Grease a 9-inch baking pan with the melted butter.
4. Place the crushed graham crackers on the bottom of the prepared baking pan.
5. Pour cheesecake mix into the baking pan.
6. Place baking pan into a larger tray with a ½-inch of water, so the 9-inch baking pan sits in water.
7. Place into the oven at 400°F (200°C) for 90 minutes.
8. Test with a toothpick in the center to make sure it's not raw in the middle. Put back in the oven for five minutes and test again if it needs more time.

Yields one 9-inch cheesecake

Poppy Seed Roll
(Ukrainian)

Variations of the popular poppy seed roll have been a mainstay of Christmas, Easter, and Shabbat celebrations in Eastern Europe for generations and have many different names, including Polish *makowiec*, Hungarian *beigli*, Viennese *Wienerbrød*, and Ukrainian *makivnyk*.

Made of a fresh yeasty, sweet bread dough with a bittersweet filling of poppy seed paste, it is rolled up like a cinnamon roll before baking so that, when it's cut, the filling creates dense swirls of dark delight. Poppy seeds feature widely in the cuisine of the former Eastern Bloc because they represent prosperity and are considered especially lucky during the holidays.

Traditionally grown in gardens and on vegetable plots, the poppies are left to go to seed before entire families go out to harvest them. These days, of course, we can buy the seed filling over the counter which makes it a whole lot easier, although we have many customers at Bea's who reminisce about the days when it wasn't so easy. This recipe is a special favorite for our Ukrainian customers and for all those nostalgic for the old country.

Known as *mohn* in Yiddish, poppy seeds have been used as a filling and a coating on bagels and breads since medieval times, as they are an excellent source of calcium and are rich in natural oils. At Bea's Bakery, our filling adds prune paste to the poppy paste for extra sweetness.

Mazel tov!

INGREDIENTS:

POPPY SEED FILLING:
- Poppy seed paste—2½ cups (547 g)
- Prune paste—2 oz. (51 g)

POPPY DOUGH:
- Fresh yeast—2 oz. (56 g)
- Granulated sugar—7 oz. (196 g)
- Salt—½ oz. (14 g)
- All-purpose shortening—2 cups (437 g)
- Patent flour—3 cups (347 g)
- Water—1 cup (240 mL)
- Whole large eggs—4 (180 mL)
- Chocolate cake crumbs—4 oz. (112 g)

TOPPING:
- Egg yolks—2 (30 mL)
- Water—1 teaspoon (5 mL)

INSTRUCTIONS:

Poppy Seed Filling:

1. Pour all ingredients into a mixing bowl.
2. Mix at first speed for 2 to 3 minutes till the mixture is smooth.

Poppy Dough:
1. Pour all ingredients into a mixing bowl except the water, eggs, and cake crumbs.
2. Mix 2 minutes till smooth.
3. Stop mixer and dust the top of the dough with flour.
4. Let the dough sit in the mixer for 15 minutes until it lifts and breaks through the flour.
5. Add the water and eggs to the mixing bowl.
6. Mix at third speed for 4 to 5 minutes till the dough is in one thick piece while mixing.
7. Roll out with flour into a rectangle on a table or work surface.
8. Spread the poppy filling in a thin layer over the dough.
9. Sprinkle chocolate cake crumbs on top of filling.
10. Roll up into a log.

Topping:
1. Beat the egg yolks and add the water. Brush the egg wash over the roll before you put it in the oven.
2. Bake at 325°F (170°C) for 45 minutes.

Yields one baking pan-sized log

Honey Cake with Variations
(Ancient and Global)

This is thought to be one of the earliest cakes in the world, revered for centuries as a symbol of immortality. Honey is one of Nature's best preservatives and was stored in jars deep in the pyramids alongside the mummified bodies of the pharaohs. The Greeks offered honey cakes to the gods and, in ancient times, Roman soldiers carried small versions into battle in case they needed something for the afterlife.

Originally made with honey and mashed-up beans (and later with barley or a wheat dough made with fresh yeast) the cakes have been adapted every which way over the years to include seeds, nuts, breadcrumbs, dried fruit, a raisin wine sauce known as *passum*, and curd cheese.

Traveling with the Arabs from the Middle East to Europe, honey cakes became sweeter still and spices from the Far East started to be added, fragrant cinnamon especially—a spice that was considered both sacred and medicinal and became so highly prized that wars were fought over it.

Once it reached the Jewish population of Europe, the moist and long-lasting honey cake quickly became a firm favorite and is often enjoyed at Rosh Hashanah, the Jewish New Year, as it symbolizes a sweet year yet to come. Honey features prominently in the Jewish religion, which began in the so-called "land of milk and honey." Each year on Rosh Hashanah, the challah bread or an apple is dipped in honey to ask God for a sweet new year.

Considered to be the fruitcake of choice from the kosher kitchen, honey cake was something Lenny's family ate every year, and it is beloved by our customers at Bea's, as it tethers them to past traditions.

INGREDIENTS:

- Vegetable oil—½ cup (120 mL)
- Whole large eggs—2 (90 mL)
- Honey—1¼ cups (300 mL)
- Water—¼ cup (60 mL)
- Granulated sugar—12 oz. (336 g)
- Baking soda—¼ oz. (7 g)
- Salt—¼ oz. (7 g)
- Cinnamon—¼ oz. (7 g)
- Rye flour—14 oz. (400 g)

INSTRUCTIONS:

1. Pour the oil, eggs, and honey into a mixing bowl.
2. Mix for 3 minutes till smooth in second speed.
3. Scrape down the sides of the bowl with a spatula.
4. Add water and mix for 1 minute till smooth.
5. Pour sugar, baking soda, salt, cinnamon, and rye flour into the bowl with the rest of the ingredients.
6. Mix for 5 minutes at third speed till the mix is smooth and warm to the touch.
7. Spray four loaf pans with baking spray.
8. Fill the prepared loaf pans evenly with the mix.
9. Bake for 55 minutes at 350°F (180°C).
10. Test the center of the cake with a toothpick. If it does not come out clean, then bake for 5 more minutes.

Yields four 12 oz. (336 g) loaves

Nigerian Pound Cake
(Nigerian)

Many think that pound cake got its name because it weighed a pound or cost one pound sterling in Britain, but those are both myths. It comes from the original eighteenth century Northern European recipe that called for a pound of each of the main ingredients—eggs, sugar, flour, and butter. The resulting cake must have been enormous.

Over the years, the quantities have reduced to regular proportions, and pound cake has come to mean any cake recipe that had four equal weights of anything.

Our Nigerian version at Bea's—as made by the women of Adaeze's tribe for generations of celebrations, including weddings and birthdays—has not four but eight ingredients of varying weights, including the delicious additions of rum, dried fruit, vanilla, and baking powder. The result is a light and fluffy, yet moist confection often referred to in Europe as Madeira cake.

The pound cake is rich and dense and has a long tradition as a dessert in the Southern states of America, too, with a variation appearing in an 1881 cookbook entitled *What Mrs. Fisher Knows About Old Southern Cooking*. The book features the 160 favorite recipes of an African American cook born a slave named Abby Fisher who moved to California after the Civil War. Although she ran her own business and won awards for her cooking, Mrs. Fisher couldn't read or write, so she dictated the recipes to friends.

Whoever makes it, for Adaeze, pound cake is something for celebrations; she and her family enjoyed one every Sunday after church. It is, she says, a cake that always made people smile.

Lenny

INGREDIENTS:

- All-purpose flour—2 cups (231 g)
- Unsalted butter—2 cups (437 g)
- Whole large eggs—5 (225 mL)
- Granulated sugar—1½ cups (304 g)
- Baking powder—1 Tablespoon (8 g)
- Vanilla—1 Tablespoon (15 mL)
- Rum—½ cup (120 mL)
- Dried fruit (any kind)—½ cup (29 g)
- Powdered sugar—½ cup (97 g)

INSTRUCTIONS:

1. Pour all ingredients except the dried fruit into a mixing bowl and mix at second speed for 5 minutes.
2. When the mixture is smooth, add the dried fruit to the bowl and mix for 1 more minute.
3. Grease a 9-inch baking pan and pour the batter in the pan.
4. Bake at 350°F (180°C) for 35 to 40 minutes, till the center is firm.

Yields one 9-inch baking tin

Napoleons
(French)

Rivalries between chefs and even countries is a longstanding tradition in cookery, and the history of the French Napoleon pastry is no exception. Some say it was created by an Italian in Naples who called it a "Napoletano" after his city, a name that was later corrupted.

Others say that greedy Napoleon Bonaparte, Emperor of France, ate such industrial quantities of it before the Battle of Waterloo that it gave him indigestion.

Another chef who claims it is his recipe was a Dane who is said to have created the zigzag pattern of icing on top of the pastry to look like the letter N for Napoleon during a state visit by the emperor to Copenhagen.

As none of these claims can now be verified, we at Bea's continue to make these deliciously flaky, layered, oblong pastries filled with custard cream for the pure pleasure of them. Our customers certainly gobble them up in industrial quantities, as they are one of our bestselling items, especially among older customers, although an entirely new generation is enjoying their discovery too.

Fiddly and a little time-consuming to make, they are nevertheless worth the effort and a plate full of fresh Napoleons is guaranteed to impress your family and friends. *Bon Appetit!*

INGREDIENTS:

PASTRY DOUGH:
- Sweet butter—1 cup (219 g)
- All-purpose flour—2 cups (231 g)
- Granulated sugar—1 Tablespoon (14 g)
- Kosher salt—½ Tablespoon (10 g)
- Cold water—10 Tablespoons (150 mL)

FILLING:
- Whole milk—2¼ cups (540 mL)
- Granulated sugar—½ cup (101 g)
- Salt—¼ teaspoon (2 g)
- Vanilla—1½ teaspoons (8 mL)
- Cornstarch—¼ cup (49 g)
- Large egg yolks—3 (45 mL)
- Sweet butter—3 Tablespoons (41 g)

GLAZE:
- Confectioners' sugar, sifted—1 cup (203 g)
- Heavy cream—¼ cup (60 mL)
- Corn syrup—½ teaspoon (3 mL)
- Melted semisweet chocolate chips—¾ oz. (21 g)

INSTRUCTIONS:

Pastry Dough:

1. Place the butter in the freezer for 10 minutes.
2. In a large mixing bowl, whisk together the flour, sugar, and salt.
3. Grate the frozen butter into the flour. (Dice the remaining end of the butter that you can't grate.) Toss the butter in the flour mixture with your hands until well coated.
4. Drizzle 6 Tablespoons of the water (90 mL) over the mixture and fold the mixture together until it clumps. Continue adding water a Tablespoon at a time, until a loose and crumbly dough forms. (It should hold when squeezed.)
5. Gently knead the dough a few times in the bowl until a cohesive mass is formed. Shape into a ½-inch-thick square and wrap tightly in plastic wrap. Chill for 1 hour.
6. On a lightly floured surface, fold and roll the chilled dough into a ½-inch-thick rectangle. Fold the dough in thirds like a letter. Turn 90 degrees. Repeat rolling, folding, and rotating three more times.
7. Fold back into thirds, wrap tightly, then chill for at least 2 hours.

Filling:

1. In a medium-sized saucepan, stir together 1½ cups (360 mL) of the milk, the sugar, salt, and vanilla bean. (If you're using vanilla extract, you'll add it at the end.) Bring to a simmer over medium heat, stirring to dissolve the sugar.
2. Meanwhile, in a medium bowl, whisk the cornstarch and egg yolks with the remaining ¾ cup (180 mL) milk until smooth and lump-free.
3. Slowly whisk about one third of the hot milk mixture into the egg mixture, then pour the egg/milk mixture back into the remaining simmering milk mixture. Bring to a boil, stirring constantly with a whisk, until the mixture thickens and the boiling bubbles reach the center of the saucepan.
4. Remove the pan from the heat and strain the filling through a fine strainer into a bowl.
5. Stir in the butter and vanilla extract. Place a piece of plastic wrap directly on top of the surface, then refrigerate until cool.

To Prepare the Pastry:

1. On a lightly floured surface, roll the chilled dough into an 11-x-14-inch rectangle about ⅛-inch thick.
2. Transfer the dough to a parchment-lined baking pan by gently folding it in half, then in quarters. Place the dough on the prepared baking pan and unfold.
3. Prick (dock) the dough all over with a fork.
4. Cover the dough with a sheet of parchment paper, then put it in the refrigerator to chill for at least 30 minutes (or as long as overnight).
5. Preheat the oven to 375°F (190°C).
6. Remove the chilled dough from the refrigerator and place another flat-bottomed baking pan on top of the parchment paper.
7. Bake the dough sandwiched between the two pans for 25 minutes. Baking the pastry under the weight of another pan will limit the vertical expansion of the layers and create an incredibly crispy pastry sheet that can carry the weight of the rich pastry cream on top. (Covered baking also allows for slow caramelizing of the dough, yielding a deep, rich flavor.)
8. Remove the top baking pan and the parchment underneath it and return the uncovered pastry to the oven to continue baking for another 15 minutes, until it's a deep golden brown and baked all the way through.
9. Remove the pastry from the oven and carefully transfer it to a rack to cool.
10. Using a serrated knife, carefully trim the edges of the baked pastry sheet to make a 10-x-12-inch rectangle.
11. Cut the rectangle into thirds to make three 10-x-4-inch strips. Select the best-looking strip of pastry and set it aside (this will become the top layer).

To Make the Glaze:

1. Place the confectioners' sugar in a bowl and stir in the cream and corn syrup.
2. Working with the melted chocolate while it's still warm (around 100 to 110°F or 37 to 43°C), transfer it to a pastry bag. (A small zip-top bag can also work here.)
3. Snip off the tip of the pastry bag or one of the corners of the zip-top bag to create a small opening about 1/16-inch wide. (You don't need to be exact here, but the opening should be quite small for best control.) Alternatively, make a cornet out of parchment.

To Assemble:

1. Working quickly, pour the white glaze over the "good-looking" reserved pastry strip, covering it completely and smoothing with an offset spatula.
2. Before the white glaze sets, pipe the chocolate glaze lengthwise onto the white-glazed strip, making parallel lines about an inch apart. With a toothpick or the tip of a paring knife, draw alternating lines perpendicularly through the chocolate stripes to pull them into a pattern.
3. Carefully place the iced pastry on a rack to dry.
4. Spread or pipe the chilled pastry cream evenly over the two remaining strips of pastry; it should be about ¾-inch thick. If you're using berries, push them down into the filling on one of the strips, then top with the other filled strip.
5. Place the iced strip on the top. Refrigerate the pastry for at least 30 minutes (or up to 12 hours) before serving; this rest will allow it to set up, making it easier to cut.
6. Slice the pastry crosswise into eight pieces, each about 1¼-inch wide. Serve chilled or warmed just slightly at room temperature.

Yields a 5-x-5-inch double filled sheet or four Napoleons

Hungarian Seven-Layer Cake
(Hungarian)

My father came from the town of Miskolc in northwest Hungary, the country's second largest city before the war. His family was very wealthy and owned an estate and a winery, and he was well-educated, speaking seven languages.

He was one of only 4,000 of the 14,000 Jews of Miskolc who survived the war and, having lost most of his family and his ancestral home to the war, he never returned to his country. Although rye bread was his favorite food after he survived, this sumptuous link to his childhood was, without a doubt, his favorite cake, and he frequently brought one home from his bakery for us all to enjoy.

Seven-layer chocolate cake is known as *Dobos Torte* or *dobostortá* in Hungary after its creator, the nineteenth century Budapest-based pastry chef József Dobos. The owner of a grand delicatessen and bakery that was the talk of the town, he donated his original recipe to the authorities so that every chef could have access to his delicious creation. Sadly, the original was lost during the Second World War, so there have been many imitations since.

Whatever the variation, however, the cake is still traditionally served for special occasions and has become a staple of Jewish life. Its richness speaks for itself—seven layers of light sponge, six layers of silky chocolate buttercream filling, then frosting on top. We have a lot to thank József Dobos for, as he is also credited with inventing buttercream—by mistake—from "spoiled butter."

Our version of his famous cake has a delicious fudge icing that we hope the master chef would approve of. A gourmet and an innovator, Dobos established the most sought-after shop in Budapest which sold everything from cakes to champagne, and he retired a wealthy man. Having become a father late in life, he married the child's mother at the age of seventy-two, dying five years later in 1924. This cake is his most famous legacy.

Lenny

INGREDIENTS:

CAKE:

- Sweet butter—1⅓ cups (310 g)
- Granulated sugar—2⅔ cups (518 g)
- Large eggs—5 (225 mL)
- Cake flour—4 cups (463 g)
- Baking powder—4 teaspoons (16 g)
- Table salt—¾ teaspoon (5 g)
- Whole milk—2 cups (480 mL)
- Vanilla—4 teaspoons (20 mL)

CHOCOLATE BUTTERCREAM FILLING:

- Sweet butter—1 cup (219 g)
- Cocoa powder, sifted—1 cup (194 g)
- Powdered sugar, sifted—8 cups (1,623 g)
- Whole milk—⅔ cup (160 mL)
- Vanilla—1½ Tablespoons (23 mL)

FUDGE ICING:

- Sweet butter—1½ cups (328 g)
- Shortening—1½ cups (328 g)
- Melted dark chocolate—1½ cups (360 mL)
- Vanilla—1 Tablespoon (15 mL)
- Powdered sugar—4 cups (777 g)

INSTRUCTIONS:

Cake Layers:

1. Grease and flour seven 9-inch square pans lined with parchment paper.
2. Cream the butter and sugar in the bowl of a stand mixer on medium speed for 5 minutes, or until light and fluffy.
3. Scrape the sides and bottom of the bowl.
4. Add the eggs one at a time, beating well after each addition.
5. Scrape the sides and bottom of the bowl again.
6. Combine the cake flour, baking powder, and salt in a separate bowl and mix with a wire whisk.
7. Combine the milk and vanilla extract in a liquid measuring cup.
8. With the mixer on low, alternate adding the flour mixture and the milk mixture, beginning and ending with the flour mixture. Beat until well blended.
9. Beat the batter for 7 minutes on medium speed.
10. Divide the batter evenly between the seven prepared pans. Tap the pans on the counter to ensure there are no air bubbles.
11. Bake for 12 minutes.
12. Cool the cakes on a cooling rack before removing from pans.

Chocolate Buttercream Filling:

1. Melt the butter in a medium saucepan over medium heat.
2. Add the cocoa powder and whisk until all the lumps are dissolved.
3. Add ¼ of the confectioners' sugar and then ¼ of the milk. Alternate until all the sugar and milk is incorporated.
4. Remove from the heat.
5. Add the vanilla extract and mix until well blended.
6. While the filling is still warm, spread it between the cake layers as you stack them; the filling will set up like fudge as it cools.
7. If the filling hardens while icing the layers, warm the filling in the microwave in 10-second intervals until the smooth, velvety texture has returned.

Chocolate Fudge Icing:

1. Cream the butter and shortening in the bowl of a stand mixer for 3 minutes. At the end of the 3 minutes, scrape the bowl extremely well.
2. Meanwhile, melt the chocolate in the microwave in 10-second intervals until smooth.
3. Add the melted chocolate to the butter and shortening with the mixer on low speed.
4. Add the vanilla and beat well.
5. Slowly add the confectioners' sugar, beating on low to ensure the sugar does not fly out of the mixing bowl.
6. After each addition of confectioners' sugar, scrape the bottom and sides of the bowl extremely well.
7. Once all the confectioners' sugar is incorporated, beat on low speed for 3 minutes.
8. Spread over the top and sides of the filled, stacked cake layers.

Yields 12 slices

Yum Yum Cakes
(Southern)

The humorously named Yum Yum Cakes are made from an old Southern recipe that is refreshingly simple compared to the Napoleons. Often served for family gatherings or potluck suppers, this sweet and decadent dessert is a basic sponge cake topped with brown sugar and a selection of granulated nuts baked to form a crunchy caramel crust.

History tells us that Yum Yums may have originated in the Netherlands, where they are a traditional festive treat and quite different from the ones we know and love. In places as far afield as Holland and Scotland, they are served as plaited fried donuts with a sugar topping or icing glaze.

They may be simple, but the melt-in-your-mouth Yum Yums we sell at Bea's certainly live up to their name, and many of our customers can't help but cry, "Yum yum," as they are eating them.

A mainstay of Bea's for over forty years, they are a hugely popular item and one we wouldn't be successful without. One older couple from Georgia who comes to the bakery often is especially fond of them as they taste like a "little piece of home."

Adaeze

INGREDIENTS:

CAKE:

- Granulated sugar—1¼ cups (254 g)
- Salt—1 pinch
- Baking powder—⅛ oz. (3 g)
- All-purpose flour—3½ oz. (98 g)
- Cake flour—10 oz. (280 g)
- All-purpose shortening—6½ oz. (182 g)
- Whole large eggs—2 (90 mL)
- Sour cream—6½ oz. (182 g)

TOPPING:

- Granulated nuts (of your choice)—6½ oz. (182 g)
- Brown sugar—7 oz. (196 g)

INSTRUCTIONS:

1. Pour all cake ingredients into a mixing bowl.
2. Mix at second speed for 2 to 3 minutes until the mix is smooth.
3. Scrape down the mixing bowl with a plastic scraper or spatula.
4. Mix at second speed for an additional 4 to 5 minutes.
5. Add the batter to a greased 8-inch cake pan.
6. In a separate bowl, mix the topping ingredients by hand and sprinkle on top of the cake.
7. Bake at 350°F (180°C) for 40 minutes.

Yields one 8-inch baking tin

Red Velvet Kola Nut Cupcakes
(Nigerian)

Of all our recipes, this "blessing cupcake" has not only become our signature baking item, but it is also one of our favorites because of its strong romantic and cultural connection to our own sweet love story. My family's heritage traces its roots back to the noble Igbo tribe in Nigeria, West Africa, from where our ancestors were first brought to America as slaves. Many of the tribe's proud traditions survived, including the offering of a sacred kola nut by a hopeful groom asking for his bride-to-be's hand from her father.

Lenny flew with me to my dad's home in Houston, Texas, and respectfully followed the strict and complicated marriage rites of presenting the nuts to him in the presence of other chiefs of our tribe as part of the so-called *Ikua aka N'uzo*, or the "Knocking on the Door" ceremony. The sweet kola nut is a symbol of humility and goodwill in Igbo culture and one that blesses a marriage with positivity, fertility, and tranquillity. Once all the prayers and rituals have been observed, including the purchase of goats for Nigerian relatives, the nut is broken and shared, often ground to a powder and added to food.

With its added kick of caffeine, it made perfect sense to us to include it in our recipe for a classic red velvet cupcake, a longstanding favorite of the South. These mouthwatering delights have the added blessing of being red, which is the color of luck, love, and joy in many faiths and cultures around the world.

Now people of all nationalities flock to Bea's for our delicious cupcakes year-round and especially for Juneteenth, which celebrates the emancipation of the slaves, Valentine's Day, and marriage proposals—because what could be more romantic? We could all do with a little more positivity and tranquillity in our lives, so this authentic offering invites everyone to have a seat at the table. We hope you feel extra blessed as you prepare and enjoy this gift from the heart for those you hold dear.

Adaeze x

INGREDIENTS:

CUPCAKES:

- All-purpose unbleached flour—2½ cups (317 g)
- Granulated sugar—1½ cups (304 g)
- Baking soda—1 teaspoon (4 g)
- Table salt—1 teaspoon (6 g)
- Cocoa powder—1 teaspoon (6 g)
- Kola nut power or tiger nut powder[1]—½ teaspoon (12 g)
- Vegetable oil—1½ cups (360 mL)
- Buttermilk—1 cup (240 mL)
- Large eggs—2 (90 mL)
- Red food coloring—1 Tablespoon (15 mL)
- Vanilla extract—1 teaspoon (5 mL)

CREAM CHEESE ICING:

- Cream cheese—8 oz. (224 g)
- Powdered sugar—4 cups (812 g)
- Splash of vanilla

INSTRUCTIONS:

Cupcakes:

1. Preheat oven to 325°F (170°C).
2. Place paper liners in a cupcake tin or grease the cups.

---

[1] If you cannot find kola or tiger nut powder, substitute with ground walnut flour, which you can find at most high-end markets.

3. In a large mixing bowl, mix the dry ingredients at second speed (cream) for 30 seconds.
4. Add the oil, buttermilk, eggs, food coloring, and vanilla; mix at second speed (cream) for 2 minutes or until smooth.
5. Scoop about 4 oz. (112 g) of batter into each cup.
6. Bake for 12 minutes.

Icing:

1. Put cream cheese, powdered sugar, and vanilla into a mixing bowl. Mix at second speed (cream) for 90 seconds until smooth and creamy.
2. Using a knife or spatula, spread on cooled cupcakes.

Yields nine 4 oz. (112 g) cupcakes

Enjoy Red Velvet Kola Nut Cupcakes for engagements, birthdays, anniversaries, or any special occasions.

Lamington Coconut Bars
(Australian)

The unusually named Lamingtons are scrumptious squares of butter sponge coated in chocolate sauce and dipped in desiccated coconut, giving them a unique texture and look. Sometimes with a filling of cream, lemon curd, or strawberry jam, they are one of our top ten bestsellers at Bea's and, even though we make at least two hundred per day, we still never make enough to please our customers.

Very few of them know that what most Americans simply call coconut bars have an even stranger history than the Napoleons. Of the many theories put forward about the origin of their name, the most plausible is that they were specially created for Lord Lamington, the eighth governor of Queensland, Australia, in the late 1800s by one of his chefs.

The governor and his wife Lady Lamington—who had a keen interest in cookery—frequently held "At Home" garden parties, also known as "Lamington Teas," at his official residence in Brisbane and his summer home at Toowoomba.

The hard-pressed cooks had to provide vast quantities of refreshments for up to a thousand guests—including "Lamington Soup," and the Lamington Cake is thought to have been invented for the purpose.

Whoever was responsible originally, there have been similar variations made all over the word from as far afield as Hungary to Mauritius, and the consensus is that—however and wherever they are made—they are one of those come-back-for-more treats that never fail to please.

INGREDIENTS:

BUTTER CAKE:

- All-purpose flour—8.5 oz. (238 g)
- Baking powder—2 teaspoons (8 g)
- Table salt—1 pinch
- Softened unsalted butter—4 oz. (112 g)
- Granulated sugar—5.5 oz. (154 g)
- Whole large eggs—2 (90 mL)
- Vanilla extract—1 teaspoon (5 mL)
- Whole milk—4 oz. (112 g)

ICING AND TOPPING:

- Powdered sugar—12 oz. (336 g)
- Unsweetened cocoa powder—2 oz. (56 g)
- Unsalted butter—2.6 oz. (73 g)
- Whole milk—8.5 oz. (238 g)
- Unsweetened coconut—7 oz. (196 g)

INSTRUCTIONS:

Butter Cake:

1. Bake the butter cake one day in advance, as it needs to spend the night in the refrigerator.
2. Preheat the oven to 350°F (180°C). Grease an 8-inch baking dish.
3. Sift together the flour, baking powder, and salt. Set aside.
4. In another bowl, beat the soft butter until creamy. Add the sugar and beat until pale and fluffy. Add one egg, beat well to incorporate, then add the second egg and the vanilla extract and beat to combine.

5. Set the mixer at the first speed. Add the flour and the milk alternatively, starting and finishing with the flour. Beat the mixture only until smooth. Do not overbeat.
6. Place the batter into the prepared baking dish and bake for 25 to 30 minutes or until a skewer inserted in the middle of the cake comes out clean. Leave the cake in the baking dish for about 10 minutes, then transfer to a wire rack and let cool completely.
7. When completely cool, wrap it well in cling film/plastic foil and refrigerate overnight.
8. The next day, cut it into even squares of about 2 inches. Place a wire rack on top of a large baking tray that will catch the possible chocolate or coconut drippings.

Chocolate Icing:
1. Sift the powdered sugar and the cocoa powder together. Set aside.
2. Melt the butter in a saucepan large enough to hold the whole icing mixture.
3. When the butter has melted, add the milk, mix, and start adding the sugar and cocoa powder mixture while whisking all the time. Add only about 1 cup at a time; whisk well and continue adding the sugar until everything is well incorporated and lump-free.

Ice Coconut Bars:
1. Pour half of the chocolate mixture into a bowl and leave the rest in the saucepan.
2. Place only one third of the coconut onto a plate.
3. Dip the bars into the chocolate mixture and coat them in coconut one by one. Work carefully (the cake squares are delicate), but rather quickly. Turn the Lamingtons in the chocolate with the help of two forks, then take the square on one fork and let the excess drain a little before you drop the cake piece into the coconut.
4. Roll the square into the coconut with the forks, transfer it to the wire rack, and continue with the next bar.
5. When the coconut gets too "dirty," and you have too many chocolate clumps in it, discard it and add fresh coconut to the plate.
6. When you finish the bars, store them in the refrigerator.

Yields one 8-inch baking tin

Lemon Bars

(American)

Although every new recipe is dreamed up by someone, it is usually a variation on something much older that has been passed down through the generations. The same is true for lemon bars, the recipe for which was submitted by a housewife to a newspaper competition in 1962.

Hopeful cook Mrs. Eleanore Mickelson won five dollars and the honor of having her recipe published in the *Chicago Tribune*. Her winning combination of a lemon curd topping and a shortbread crust captured the hearts—and stomachs—of America and has been a sugary treat for millions ever since.

Her recipe was a clever new idea based on an old theme, because shortbread has been around since it was first created in Scotland in the twelfth century. Mary, Queen of Scots, was said to be so addicted in the sixteenth century she had her chefs refine the recipe to make it crumblier and "shorter."

It was Mrs. Mickelson's addition of a lemon curd topping that won her the prize. Lemon curd was a British invention in which acidic lemon juice was poured into cream to make curds that separated from the whey through a muslin sieve. The first known recipe was published in 1844 by another rather wonderfully named woman: Lady Charlotte Campbell Berry. Lemon curd or lemon cheese, as it was sometimes called, was sweetened with sugar from a solid conical loaf of sugar that was broken off and grated or melted.

We introduced lemon bars to Bea's Bakery, and it is another popular item. Our recipe is far less taxing than the Lady Campbell Berry's and calls for lemon juice and zest, 1½ cups of granulated sugar (no need to find a loaf), and a couple of eggs.

In a little over an hour, you will have two dozen two-inch bars that you can enjoy with a toast to Mrs. Mickelson.

INGREDIENTS:

CRUST:

- All-purpose flour—1 cup (127 g)
- Granulated sugar—¼ cup (51 g)
- Salt—1 pinch
- Unsalted butter—4 oz. (112 g)

FILLING:

- Whole large eggs—1½ (68 mL)
- Granulated sugar—1½ cups (304 g)
- Lemon zest—1 Tablespoon (12 g)
- Lemon juice—½ cup (120 mL)
- All-purpose flour—½ cup (63 g)

INSTRUCTIONS:

1. Sift the flour, sugar, and salt into a large bowl. Using two knives or your fingertips (recommended), cut in the butter until the mixture clumps up to the size of small peas. Press the mixture into the bottom of a 9-x-13-inch baking pan, and about ¾-inch up the sides of the pan to keep the filling from leaking during baking.
2. Bake at 325°F (170°C) for about 20 to 30 minutes, until golden brown. Set aside to cool.
3. To make the filling (you can do this as you are baking the crust), whisk eggs and sugar together until well combined.

4. Add the zest and juice; whisk well. Sift the flour over the top and stir until well blended.

5. Pour the filling over the cooled crust. Bake until set, about 30 to 35 minutes. (They should be slightly jiggly.)

6. Let the pan cool completely before cutting up into bars. Dust with confectioners' sugar, if desired.

Yields twenty-four 2-inch bars

Nigerian Coconut Candy Bars
(Nigerian)

Street food has long been a tradition in Adaeze's ancestral home of Nigeria, especially during masquerades and fiestas where people take to the streets to dance, socialize, eat, drink, and have fun.

Coconut candy is one of the most popular types of street food and is often sold in glass jars before being scooped into paper cups or hollowed out coconut shells. In essence, it is toasted flakes of fresh coconut with a little sugar and salt added and can be eaten by the handful, or sprinkled over ice cream and garri, which is baked cassava root flour. It can also be used as a basis for coconut balls.

It's not surprising that coconuts feature a lot in Nigerian cooking as they grow in abundance there. The tropical palm known as the "Tree of Life" is especially revered in Africa. And for good reason. It provides milk, edible white flesh that provides nutritious fats, a woody husk of a shell that doubles as a bowl, branches that can be used for thatching, and quality wood for building from its trunk.

Adaeze's coconut candy bars are created in homage to the Tree of Life; they feature grated coconut, cinnamon, sugar, and vanilla mixed together with a little baking powder.

Nuo nk oma! (which is Igbo for "Cheers!")

Adaeze

INGREDIENTS:

- Non-sweet, grated coconut—2 cups (269 g)
- Powdered cinnamon—1 teaspoon (3 g)
- Granulated sugar—1½ cups (304 g)
- Baking powder—¼ teaspoon (1 g)
- Room temperature water—½ cup (120 mL)
- Vanilla—2 teaspoons (10 mL)

INSTRUCTIONS:

1. Pour all ingredients into a mixing bowl.
2. Mix at second speed for 5 minutes or until the mix is smooth.
3. Grease an 8-inch baking pan.
4. Pour batter into baking pan.
5. Bake at 350°F (180°C) for 35 minutes or until the center is firm.

Yields one 8-inch baking pan

Pecan Bars
(Southern)

Pecan pie is a timeless staple of Southern cooking but can be fiddly and time-consuming to make. Making pecan bars, however, is easier than pie, and they pack all the same flavor and crunch. You can also make them in bite-size pieces for parties, picnics, or simply a delicious snack to eat at home. What's not to like?

The recipes for pecan pie date back to the middle 1800s when pecan trees—a relative of the deciduous hickory—were first domesticated in the Southern states of Texas, Georgia, New Mexico, and northern Mexico. Eaten by Native Americans for centuries, they were discovered by Spanish explorers in the sixteenth century who called then "wrinkle nuts" because of their natural distinctive corrugation. Although the pecan is officially a kind of fruit, not a nut, it is designated the state nut of several other states, including California, although arguments about its pronunciation are debated worldwide. "Pea-cahn" is most commonly used in the States, but in England it is "pee-can."

No matter how it is pronounced, it is universally agreed that the ridged pecan is a large and versatile nut full of goodness with a buttery richness. It can be eaten raw or roasted, produces an edible oil, and can be churned into butter. The wood of the tree, often sold as hickory chips, is used extensively for barbecues and for smoking fish and meat and is also used for furniture making and carpentry.

High in calories and a rich source of vitamins and dietary fiber, pecans are predominantly fat but of the polyunsaturated or monosaturated variety, which is better for our health. So you can make these scrumptious bars with their sweet nutty topping to your heart's delight.

INGREDIENTS:

- All-purpose flour—3 cups (381 g)
- Granulated sugar—½ cup (101 g)
- Salt—½ teaspoon (2 g)
- Unsalted butter—1 cup (219 g)
- Corn syrup—1½ cups (360 mL)
- Granulated sugar—1½ cups (304 g)
- Whole large eggs—4 (180 mL)
- Melted margarine—3 Tablespoons (41 g)
- Vanilla—1½ teaspoons (8 mL)
- Chopped pecans—2½ cups (320 g)

INSTRUCTIONS:

1. Prepare a greased 8-x-15-inch baking pan.
2. Combine flour, ½ cup sugar (101 g), and salt in a large bowl. Cut in 1 cup (230 g) of unsalted butter until the mixture resembles coarse crumbs. Sprinkle the mixture evenly over the prepared pan and press in firmly to make a crust.
3. Bake in a preheated oven at 400°F (200°C) degrees for 20 minutes.
4. Meanwhile, mix the corn syrup, 1½ cups (360 mL) sugar, eggs, 3 Tablespoons (45 mL) margarine, and vanilla together in a large bowl until smooth. Stir in chopped pecans; spread the filling evenly over the baked crust in the pan.
5. Bake at 350°F (180°C) for 25 minutes. Allow to cool completely in the pan on a wire rack before slicing into bars.

Yields one tray of sixteen bars (cut four by four)

Flourless Chocolate Cake
(Italian)

This unbelievably rich and creamy dessert isn't just for those who have food intolerances or for whom religious holidays forbid gluten and grains; it's for anyone who likes their cake to melt on their tongue before they've even had a chance to swallow.

Without any flour or other starchy meal, it is made from melted bittersweet chocolate, butter, eggs, sugar, cocoa powder, and a teaspoon of vanilla, giving it the consistency of fudge with a slight crust. The cocoa powder is the secret weapon, adding a concentrated chocolatey flavor to counter the bitterness of the dark chocolate without making it too sickly sweet.

The popularity of this cake stretches back to the last century and takes us to Europe again, where it is better known as a *torte* or *torta*. Believed to have been made especially for Princess Elena of Montenegro, "the bride with a tender heart," when she became queen of Italy in 1900, it was created by pastry chefs in Ferrara, Italy, in her honor.

Not surprisingly then, for a dessert based on a true-life love affair, this cake is especially popular for Valentine's Day, when it is often served with raspberries, strawberries, berry coulis, a dollop of crème fraiche, or vanilla ice cream. But any chocolate lover would be tempted by this beauty. Better still, it is relatively easy to make and a brilliant first start for those just beginning their baking journeys.

INGREDIENTS:

- Dark bittersweet chocolate—15 oz. (420 g)
- Unsalted butter—15 oz. (420 g)
- Whole large eggs—7 (315 mL)
- Granulated sugar—18 oz. (504 g)
- Cocoa powder—6 oz. (168 g)
- Vanilla extract—1 teaspoon (5 mL)

INSTRUCTIONS:

1. Add the chocolate and butter into a pot.
2. Heat the pot on a stove over medium heat and stir with a wire whisk carefully till fully melted; be sure not to overheat.
3. With a mixer at second speed, mix the eggs and sugar for 5 minutes or till completely whipped and fluffy.
4. Meanwhile, sift the cocoa powder with a strainer.
5. After the eggs are whipped, fold in the melted chocolate and butter, and mix with a hand wire whisk till smooth.
6. Then add the cocoa powder and vanilla to the whipped eggs mixture and mix with a handheld wire whisk till completely smooth again.
7. Pour into two 8-inch baking pans coated with baking spray.
8. Bake at 375°F (190°C) for 45 minutes.

Yields two 8-inch cakes

CHAPTER 3

Cookies

Ube Cookies
(Filipino)

Whenever we set up the display shelves in Bea's Bakery, we're always grateful to these ube cookies for their distinctively purple hue that add a splash of color to the trays and trays of baked goods that very often feature tones of mostly cream and brown. No wonder they feature so frequently in our customers' Instagram and TikTok posts.

The word *ube* means "tuber" in the Filipino Tagalog language. Related to its cousin, the sweet potato, this iconic and beloved root vegetable first traveled to the Philippines from Southeast Asia and became a culturally significant part of its heritage. A plant that thrives in almost every climate and situation, it also came to represent Filipino adaptability and resilience. As such, it has been a staple and a comfort food in the country's culture for centuries.

These popular Filipino-American treats are also known as "purple yam cookies" and have a crunchy exterior and a chewy interior with a distinctively nutty flavor and a vanilla edge. The technicolor ube is full of antioxidants, vitamins, and fiber so are—in theory—very good for us, except that the sugar, butter, eggs, and white chocolate chips in this recipe might just negate some of that goodness if overindulged.

No matter how many you wolf down in one sitting, we know that you'll love them, so, as the Filipinos would say, *Magsaya*. Enjoy!

INGREDIENTS:

- Softened unsalted butter—1 cup (219 g)
- Granulated sugar—½ cup (101 g)
- Light brown sugar—¾ cup (152 g)
- Whole large eggs—2 (90 mL)
- Ube extract—2 teaspoons (10 mL)
- Ube jam or ube spread—½ cup (120 mL)
- All-purpose flour—2½ cups (317 g)
- Cornstarch—1 Tablespoon (12 g)
- Baking powder—1½ Tablespoons (18 g)
- Baking soda—½ teaspoon (6 g)
- Salt—¼ teaspoon (5 g)
- White chocolate chips—8.5 oz. (240 g)

INSTRUCTIONS:

1. Preheat your oven to 400°F (200°C).
2. Cream butter and sugars with a mixer (using the paddle attachment) until light and fluffy.
3. Add eggs and ube extract, and mix until incorporated.
4. Add the ube jam and mix until smooth.
5. Add the flour, cornstarch, baking powder, baking soda, and salt. Mix until just combined.
6. Mix in the white chocolate chips.

7. Divide the dough into eight equal pieces. Form into tall balls and add more white chocolate chips on top.
8. Chill for about 15 minutes.
9. Put the eight cookie dough pieces equal distance apart on an 8-x-15-inch baking pan with baking paper.
10. Bake for 12 to 13 minutes or until slightly golden on the sides.
11. Let cool for 20 minutes before serving.

Yields eight cookies

Chinese Cookies
(Jewish / Chinese)

The friendship between the Chinese and the Jewish communities stretches back decades and was never more evident than during the Second World War, when refugees, fleeing from the Nazis and barred from most other countries, were openly welcomed by the Chinese in Shanghai.

The city had a long association with Jews who'd fled from persecution in the Middle East and created a thriving and wealthy community there. Its members helped fund the 20,000 or so Jews who arrived, but many still lived alongside the local Chinese, whose food and traditions of family and religious dedication they came to appreciate.

This crumbly cookie with a nutty flavor and a dollop of sweet fudge frosting in the center was one of the recipes that emerged from that remarkable cultural exchange. The almond cookie has long been a favorite in Jewish cooking, so it's a little surprising that it is frequently served instead of a fortune cookie at the end of Chinese meals in American restaurants. Often, they add a blanched almond for decoration.

No one knows where the idea came from to add a drop of chocolate fudge, ganache, or even a Hershey kiss to the center, but, like all recipes, they morph and alter with time and experimentation until something becomes so popular that it sticks. This is one of those recipes. Our customers certainly enjoy the delicious combination of nuts and sugar, chocolate and vanilla, that is perfect with a morning cup of coffee, and few knew of its interesting historical origins—until now.

INGREDIENTS:

COOKIES:

- Granulated sugar—2 cups (406 g)
- Almond paste—½ cup (151 g)
- Unsalted butter—2 cups (437 g)
- Whole large eggs—3 (135 mL)
- All-purpose flour—2½ cups (317 g)
- Baking powder—3 teaspoons (12 g)
- Table salt—½ Tablespoon (10 g)
- Vanilla extract—1 teaspoon (5 mL)

FUDGE FROSTING:

- Vegetable shortening—½ cup (115 g)
- Fudge base—¼ cup (57.5 g)

INSTRUCTIONS:

1. Add the sugar, almond paste, and butter to a mixing bowl.
2. Mix at second speed for 5 minutes or until smooth.
3. Add eggs, flour, baking powder, salt, and vanilla to the bowl and mix for 5 minutes or until smooth again.
4. Roll into a log and cut ½-inch thick slices.
5. Put the cookie dough pieces equal distance apart on an 8-x-15-inch baking pan with baking paper.
6. Bake at 350°F (180°C) for 12 to 13 minutes.
7. Mix shortening and fudge base in a bowl with a wire whisk till it reaches a frosting consistency.
8. Add the frosting to a pastry bag with a round hole as a tip to squirt out of.
9. Decorate the center of each cookie with the frosting.

Yields ten to twelve 3 oz. (84 g) cookies

Rainbow Cookies
(Italian American)

More of a cake than a cookie, these tri-colored delights were first created by patriotic Italian American bakers more than a century ago to celebrate their national flag of red, white, and green stripes.

They have since been adopted by people of all nationalities and creeds for their cheerful appearance and the fact that their red and green colors also mimic those of Christmas.

As Jewish immigrants often lived alongside Italian settlers when they first came to America, the Jewish community adopted them as a celebration cookie, and they soon became a staple of Jewish cuisine, especially on Shabbat morning. They're especially popular with children, who are attracted by their vivid hues, and often are served in synagogues. To keep them kosher, margarine is substituted for butter, and for Hannukah the colors are changed to blue and white.

The gay community, frequently represented by a rainbow flag, were also quick to adopt these sweet treats and creating them in various colors, making them truly multicultural across all divides.

Lenny's dad first started making these old-school favorites in his New York bakery, and they've been sold in his family bakeries ever since. Full of almond flavor with an added coating of chocolate, they take a little time to make, but you'll be glad when you do because—just like the feeling we get whenever we see a rainbow—these will brighten up a rainy day.

INGREDIENTS:

- Granulated sugar—1 cup (194 g)
- Almond paste—8 oz. (224 g)
- Softened sweet butter—12 oz. (336 g)
- Whole large eggs—3 (135 mL)
- Whole milk—¼ cup (60 mL)
- Almond extract—2 teaspoons (10 mL)
- All-purpose flour—2 cups (254 g)
- Red food coloring—¼ teaspoon (1 mL)
- Green food coloring—¼ teaspoon (1 mL)
- Raspberry jam—½ cup (120 mL)
- Melted semisweet chocolate chips—1½ cups (454 g)

INSTRUCTIONS:

1. Preheat the oven to 325°F (170°C), and grease three 9-x-13-inch quarter sheet pans with cooking spray, then line each with parchment.
2. In a stand mixer fitted with the paddle attachment, combine the sugar, almond paste, and 4 oz. (112 g) of the butter. Mix until smooth and lump-free, being sure to break down the almond paste as best you can. Add the remaining 8 oz. (224 g) of butter and continue to mix until smooth, scraping down the sides of the bowl as needed.
3. Separate the yolks from the whites of the eggs.
4. Gradually add the egg yolks, followed by the milk and almond extract. Mix until combined. Add the flour and slowly mix until combined, scraping down the sides of the bowl as needed. Once the flour is incorporated, set aside.
5. In a separate bowl, whip the egg whites until they form stiff, fluffy peaks. Fold the whipped egg whites into the flour mixture to form a smooth batter, then divide equally between 3 bowls.
6. Stir the red food coloring into the first bowl of batter until evenly pink, then stir the green coloring into the second bowl of batter until evenly

green, leaving the third bowl untouched. Keeping the batters separate, evenly spread them into the 3 greased and parchment-lined quarter sheet pans and bake, rotating halfway through, until set or for 10 to 12 minutes. Then let cool completely.

7. Once cooled, spread half of the jam to cover the surface of the green cake and place the undyed layer, making sure the parchment is discarded, directly on top, sandwiching the jam. Repeat this step by spreading the remaining jam on top of the undyed layer and placing the pink layer directly on top of it, discarding the parchment.

8. Cover the cake with plastic wrap and top with another sheet pan. Weigh down the layers with heavy plates or cans and refrigerate for at least 4 hours or overnight.

9. Remove the weights and plastic wrap. Spread half of the melted chocolate over the top of the cake and refrigerate until set, about 30 minutes.

10. Once solid, flip the cake onto a cutting board, discarding the bottom layer of parchment, and spread the remaining melted chocolate in an even layer over the surface.

11. Return to the refrigerator and chill until set, about 30 minutes.

12. Once set, trim into a 7½-x-10½-inch cake form, reserving all trim for snacking. Cut the cake into 1½-inch squares, then serve.

Yields forty rainbow cookies

Butter Cookies
(Danish)

People often confuse Danish butter cookies with shortbread because they are so similar, but shortbread has a far crumblier consistency than the all-butter, melt-in-your-mouth Danish version, which adds eggs to make them softer. Either way, these cookies are simple delights that need no adornment.

Danish butter cookies, known as *sablés* in France (a word that means "sandy" in reference to their texture), use similar amounts of butter to shortbread but add more sugar and flour. This allows them to crumble less and hold their shape, especially if being piped into squares, swirls, or even patterns mimicking pretzels. Because of their attractive look, taste, and durability, they have become a holiday cookie of choice for Christmas and for the Chinese Lunar New Year.

The reason the Danes got to claim these cookies as their own dates to the creation of Lurpak, a quality brand of butter in Denmark first sold in 1901. Made from cow's milk mixed with rapeseed oil for spread-ability, the global success of Lurpak led to a company called Royal Dansk establishing itself in the 1960s after merging with another Danish baked goods company whose butter cookies were bestsellers in China and Hong Kong. Royal Dansk still make and market their own brand of butter cookies and sell more than 25,000 tons of them a year in what have become iconic blue tins.

Lovely as the tinned versions are, the pleasure of a homemade cookie can't be beaten, from the smell of it fresh from the oven to the warmth of the cookie dough on your tongue. *Jubel!*

INGREDIENTS:

- Granulated sugar—1½ cups (304 g)
- Butter—2½ cups (547 g)
- Table salt—1 pinch
- Vanilla extract—½ teaspoon (3 mL)
- Pastry flour—2¼ cups (286 g)
- Whole large eggs—2 (90 mL)

INSTRUCTIONS:

1. Combine sugar, butter, salt, and vanilla in a mixing bowl.
2. Mix at second speed for 5 minutes till all combined.
3. Add in pastry flour and whole large eggs.
4. Mix at second speed for 5 minutes till dough is all combined.
5. Roll the dough out to ¼-inch thickness with a sprinkle of any flour on the table so it does not stick.
6. Cut out with your favorite cookie cutters to make your favorite-shaped cookies.
7. Bake at 350°F (180°C) for 12 minutes.

Yields twelve 3-to-4-inch cookies

Mexican Wedding Cookies/Snowballs *(Mexican / Ukrainian)*

The first Christmas after Russia invaded Ukraine in 2022, a couple wandered into Bea's Bakery and gazed in wonder at the myriad cakes and cookies on display. When they spoke, we could tell from their accents that they were from Eastern Europe.

Although we understood them, we didn't know what they meant when, with hope in their eyes, they asked us, "Do you sell Snowballs?" They explained that they were a traditional treat in their home country of Ukraine—sweet globes of cookie dough flavored with vanilla and nuts and rolled in powdered sugar to resemble snow.

Their faces full of emotion, the couple revealed that their home had been destroyed in the early days of the conflict and, in fear for their lives, they'd fled to relatives in California. This would be their first Christmas far from their country, and they craved this sweet reminder of home.

Promising to do some research, we discovered that Snowballs are also known as Russian tea cakes and are remarkably similar to the Mexican Wedding Cookies we knew and loved so well in America. Further research revealed that the sweet and easy recipe may have originated in medieval Arab cooking and then migrated into Europe via the trade routes, before traveling to Mexico with Spanish conquistadors and European missionaries. There, it was embraced for weddings celebrations and fiestas with the Mexicans using locally sourced pecan nuts instead of walnuts, hazelnuts, or almonds.

Now made the world over and with a variety of different names, from Butterballs to Pecan Sandies, these powdery white confections melt in the mouth and are the epitome of joy. And they certainly brought smiles to the faces of the displaced Ukrainian couple when we agreed to add them to our menu specially for them.

INGREDIENTS:

COOKIES:
- Brown sugar—3½ oz. (100 g)
- Table salt—1 pinch
- Milk powder—¼ oz. (7 g)
- Shortening (high ratio)—6 oz. (168 g)
- Sweet butter—¼ Tablespoon (3 g)
- Vanilla—1 splash
- Cake flour—6½ oz. (182 g)
- Granulated walnuts—1 oz. (28 g)
- Whole large egg—1 (45 mL)

TOPPING:
- Powdered sugar—1 cup (194 g)

INSTRUCTIONS:

1. Preheat your oven to 350°F (180°C).
2. In a mixing bowl, cream together the brown sugar, salt, milk powder, shortening, butter, and vanilla for 30 seconds.
3. Add in the cake flour, walnuts, and egg. Cream together for 30 seconds until well-mixed.
4. On a floured surface, shape the dough into logs.
5. Cut into finger-length pieces or use a 2-oz. (56 g) scoop.

6. Place dough on a parchment paper–covered or oiled baking pan.
7. Bake for 15 minutes.
8. Sift powdered sugar over the baked cookies for toppings.

Yields twelve 2-oz. (56 g) cookies

Enjoy Mexican Wedding Cookies for celebrations and after-school snacks.

Triple Chocolate Cookies
(American)

These cookies are so yummy that they fly off the shelves at Bea's Bakery. Some of our clients come in for them so often they claim they must now be 50 percent cookie! Thought to have originated in New York, these gooey delights are crunchy on the outside but soft in the middle, with melted white chocolate chips all wrapped up warm in a bittersweet chocolate and cocoa powder blanket. What's not to like?

Super easy to make and baked in just thirteen minutes once prepared, the secret is in the two types of sugar, a good cocoa powder, and two different types of chocolate chips for contrast—and, remember, we have Ruth Graves Wakefield to thank for those.

While we're on the subject of history, did you know the word *cookie* comes from the Dutch word *koekje* meaning "little cake"? Cookies were first introduced to America by the Europeans and were thought to have originated in Persia in the seventh century. Some food historians have speculated that they started as small dollops of test cakes, puddled onto a brick or tile and placed on an open fire to test the temperature.

The size and ease of them must have appealed, because people the world over have been making cookies ever since, even though they call them anything from *biscuits* (English) to *keks* (German), *gallettini* (Maltese) to *šušenka* (Czech).

Harder versions of what we know as cookies became very popular as people started to travel more, as they were easy to transport and kept well. The so-called "hardtack" was a staple for sailors exploring the high seas and could last for years.

Through all these changes and modifications, the basic recipe for cookies has never really changed and always features flour, sugar, and some kind of fat. Well, as the saying goes, if it ain't broke, don't fix it!

INGREDIENTS:

- Unsalted butter—3⅛ oz. (88 g)
- Margarine—3⅛ oz. (88 g)
- Brown sugar—10 oz. (280 g)
- Granulated sugar—2½ oz. (70 g)
- Whole large eggs—2 (90 mL)
- All-purpose flour—11 oz. (308 g)
- Cocoa powder—3 oz. (84 g)
- Baking soda—⅓ oz. (9 g)
- Salt—1 pinch
- Bittersweet chocolate chips—1½ oz. (42 g)
- White chocolate chips—1½ oz. (42 g)
- Vanilla—1 small splash

INSTRUCTIONS:

1. Add butter, margarine, brown sugar, and granulated sugar into a mixing bowl.
2. Mix at second speed for 2 minutes.
3. Scrape down the sides and bottom of the bowl with a plastic scraper.
4. Add eggs into mixing bowl and mix at second speed for 2 minutes.
5. Scrape down the bowl with a plastic scraper again.
6. Add the flour, cocoa powder, baking soda, and salt, and mix at second speed for 2 to 3 minutes until the mix is smooth.
7. Add both types of chocolate chips and the vanilla and mix at first speed for 1 minute till all combined.

8. By hand or with an ice cream scoop, make 3 oz. (84 g) balls and add to a cookie sheet with baking paper.
9. Flatten the dough balls slightly on the cookie sheet.
10. Bake at 350°F (180°C) for 13 minutes.

Yields twelve to fourteen 3 oz. (84 g) cookies

Spritz Cookies
(German)

This is another buttery holiday staple and an unsung hero that dates back centuries. Better still, spritz cookies give bakers the bonus of allowing them to become more creative or even adventurous, so they're especially fun to make with children.

The cookie's unusual name comes from the German word *spritzen*—to spurt or squirt—as the dough was traditionally squirted from a pastry bag with a star or other shaped nozzle. These days, there are cookie presses that do the job quickly and effortlessly without so much mess. They work by forcing the dough through a cylinder using a plunger and squirting it out the other end through different patterned discs. We at Bea's still love the traditional way, which is not only enjoyable but becomes a sort of old-fashioned mindfulness practice with its need for a steady hand, some mental focus, and a sense of rhythm.

In Germany during advent and Christmastime, *spritzgebäck* or *dressiergebäck* (dressing biscuits) are a popular baked treat often sold at Christmas markets iced, dusted with icing sugar, or covered in sprinkles. They come in all shapes and sizes and are often fashioned into little fir trees, baubles, wreaths, snowflakes, and candy canes.

There are myriad flavor variations, too, including recipes featuring chocolate, ginger, pumpkin, or even cream cheese. Food colorings are widely used to make green and red cookies that echo the colors of the season.

Spritz cookies have also been popular in Scandinavia for centuries and are called *spritsa kakor* in Sweden, where guests are traditionally served seven different shapes. In the Netherlands, *botersprits* often have a higher than usual fat content and a denser dough to keep the taste warm during the cold winter months.

As with all baked goods that are made with care, they are universally loved and summon up the joy of Christmases past, although you don't have to wait until December to enjoy them. Happy holidays!

INGREDIENTS:

- Granulated sugar—1 cup (203 g)
- Almond paste—1 cup (240 mL)
- Whole large eggs—4 (180 mL)
- Unsalted butter—2 cups (480 mL)
- Vanilla extract—½ teaspoon (3 mL)
- All-purpose flour—1 cup (127 g)
- Cake flour—1 cup (127 g)

INSTRUCTIONS:

1. Add sugar and almond paste into a mixing bowl. Mix at second speed for 8 minutes till smooth.
2. Add eggs and mix again at second speed for 1 minute till smooth.
3. Add the rest of the ingredients to the bowl and mix by hand till combined.
4. Add the batter to a pastry bag and "spritz" into desired 2-inch shapes on a cookie sheet with baking paper.
5. Bake at 350°F (180°C) for 12 minutes till golden brown.

Yields twenty to twenty-five 3 oz. (84 g) cookies

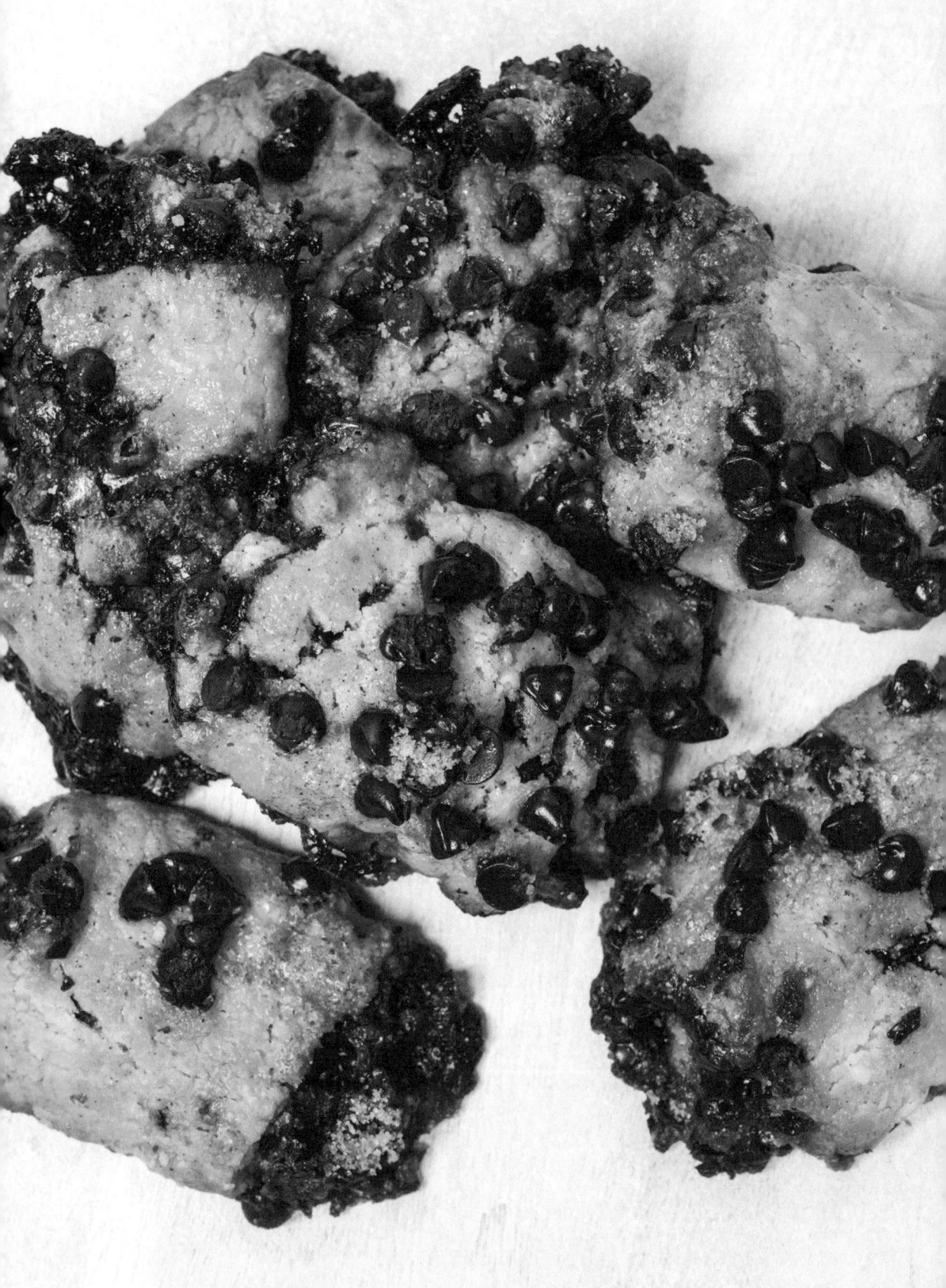

Chocolate Rugelach
(Polish / Jewish)

The word *rugelach* comes from the Yiddish and translates to "little twists," which perfectly describes this irresistible pastry which has a strong historical connection with the Ashkenazi Jews and the diaspora.

Originally a simple dough filled with cream cheese or sour cream—cheap ingredients familiar to those who kept livestock—it has been added to over the years as nuts, spices, jam, seeds, and fruit became more readily available. Said to have been inspired by *kipfel*, the Viennese pastries created to mark the end of a two-month siege of Vienna by the Ottoman Turks in the late 1600s, these croissant-shaped little bites of deliciousness are enough to make anyone celebrate.

Our chocolate rugelach is one of our bestsellers at Bea's and for good reason. Each batch features two cups of chocolate added as a topping to the sweet, moist dough full of cream cheese, eggs, sugar, and milk. Could there be anything more comforting?

INGREDIENTS:

DOUGH:
- Cream cheese—3 cups (656 g)
- Unsalted butter—2½ cups (547 g)
- Granulated sugar—4 oz. (112 g)
- Whole large eggs—5 (225 mL)
- Whole milk—1 cup (240 mL)
- All-purpose flour—5½ cups (698 g)
- Vanilla extract—1 teaspoon (5 mL)

FILLING & TOPPING:
- Granulated sugar—1 cup (203 g)
- Cocoa powder—2 oz. (56 g)
- Melted butter—1 cup (240 mL)
- Melted confectioners' chocolate—1 cup (240 mL)
- Semisweet chocolate chips—1 cup (302 g)

INSTRUCTIONS:

Dough:

1. Add all the dough ingredients into a mixing bowl.
2. Mix at second speed till smooth.
3. Place the dough onto any baking pan with a dusting of flour on the bottom of the pan.
4. Refrigerate dough for 2 hours until it's firm.

Filling & Topping:

1. Mix the sugar and cocoa powder together in a separate bowl.
2. On a floured surface, roll the dough out to about ½-inch thick.
3. Brush the dough with melted butter, then spread the chocolate, chocolate chips, and cinnamon sugar over the dough.
4. Cut all the dough on the floured surface into 1-inch wide and 1½-inch long strips.
5. Roll up each strip into a small rectangle ball and then place on a cookie sheet with baking paper standing up.
6. Bake at 325°F (170°C) for 25 minutes.

Yields one pan of rugelach, about thirty small rolls

Gluten-Free Version:

⋄ Substitute the same amount of all-purpose flour with whole grain, gluten-free flour.

Sugar-Free Cinnamon Raisin Rugelach (Jewish)

Cinnamon spice features in many of our recipes for a very good reason—it has become so beloved in baking for its rich and fragrant flavor that harks back to ancient times in Egypt and China. This exotic and rare "food of the gods" was considered an aphrodisiac, a health tonic, and an antiseptic and was kept in glass cases or ceremonially burned on funeral pyres.

Yet when we liberally sprinkle cinnamon powder into a filling or mix, we rarely give a thought to the effort involved in growing and harvesting it in countries like Sri Lanka and Vietnam. Once the cinnamon bushes are mature enough, workers strip the leggy side branches and soak them in water. Hours later they begin to peel thin strips of the bark away by hand, a labor-intensive task. Once stripped, these "quills" curl in on themselves to produce sticks that are exported around the world, either whole or ground to a fine powder.

With Sri Lanka (then Ceylon) producing the most and the best quality, both wild and in commercial plantations, cinnamon became a vital piece of international trade. Portuguese, Italian, Dutch, and British traders were the dominant partners since the eighteenth century and even fought wars over it.

The spice was so highly prized that it was considered a suitable gift to give to a king in the Far East. In Greece it was used for digestive problems and to treat the flu. And in the Jewish religion, it was an offering at the altar in Jerusalem.

This recipe for cinnamon raisin rugelach, a traditional crescent-shaped Jewish pastry with a name that originated in Poland, has a healthy two oz. of cinnamon, along with raisins, butter, cream cheese, eggs, flour, sweetener, and vanilla. So, when you sprinkle your powdered cinnamon into the food processor, have a thought for the men and women sitting on a floor on the other aside of the world, carefully peeling bark so that you can have a little taste of their work.

INGREDIENTS:

DOUGH:
- Cream cheese—3 cups (656 g)
- Unsalted butter—20 oz. (560 g)
- Monk fruit sugar—4 oz. (112 g)
- Whole large eggs—5 (225 mL)
- Milk—1 cup (240 mL)
- All-purpose flour—5½ cups (698 g)
- Vanilla—1 teaspoon (5 mL)

FILLING & TOPPING:
- Monk fruit sugar—1 cup (203 g)
- Cinnamon—2 oz. (56 g)
- Melted butter—1 cup (240 mL)
- Raisins—1 cup (120 g)

INSTRUCTIONS:

Dough:

1. Add the cream cheese, butter, and monk fruit sugar into a mixing bowl.
2. Mix at second speed for 3 to 4 minutes, till the mix is smooth.
3. Add the eggs, milk, flour, and vanilla into the mixing bowl with the other ingredients.
4. Mix at second speed for 2 to 3 minutes till all ingredients are combined and smooth.
5. Refrigerate the dough for 2 hours until firm.

Filling & Topping:

1. Mix the monk fruit sugar and cinnamon together.
2. On a floured surface, roll the dough out to about ½-inch thick.
3. Brush the dough with melted butter, then spread the raisins and cinnamon sugar over the dough.
4. Cut all the dough on the floured surface into 1-inch wide and 1½-inch long strips.
5. Roll all the dough on the floured surface into a rectangle ball and place on a cookie sheet with baking paper.
6. Bake at 325°F (170°C) for 25 minutes.

Yields one pan of rugelach, thirty small rolls

Nigerian Ground Nut Cookies
(Nigerian)

In Adaeze's ancestral lands, ground nuts are widely used in cooking as they are relatively easy to grow and provide a good source of protein, vitamins, antioxidants, and oil. Their production has a long and rich history dating back to precolonial times and forms a vital part of the economy.

From the same family as peanuts, the groundnut was first imported to Africa in the fifteenth century by the Spanish conquistadores of Bolivia and Peru. It became so important as a cash crop to the Nigerians that it featured on a national stamp and helped create a phenomenon known as the groundnut pyramids—vast pyramid-like structures created from thousands of sacks of harvested groundnuts.

Building symmetrical rows of pyramids as far as the eye could see was the idea of one of the nut's main traders in Nigeria in the early 1900s, and it proved to be an impressive and eye-catching way of storing the nuts until they could be shipped as far afield as India and the United Kingdom. As more pyramids sprang up all over the country, they started to attract tourists and became synonymous with wealth and success.

Groundnuts also played an important role in Nigerian folklore and were said to represent female wealth, perhaps because of the curvaceous shape of the husk. Nigeria is now the largest producer of groundnuts in Africa and the third largest in the world, so it's not surprising that this simple yet delicious cookie is a popular treat there too, sometimes "spritzed" out of pastry bags (much like the German Spritz Cookie recipe on page 115) to create shapes that have relevance to African society.

Often called *kulikuli*, they can be made savory or sweet, and some bakers even add a dash of chili powder for extra heat.

INGREDIENTS:

- Powdered sugar—1½ cups (291 g)
- Ground nuts (fine powder)—1½ cups (191 g)
- Almond paste—1½ cups (331 g)
- All-purpose flour—4 oz. (112 g)
- Sweet butter—4 oz. (112 g)
- Egg whites—2 (30 mL)
- Sliced almonds—½ cup (55 g)

INSTRUCTIONS:

1. Add sugar, ground nuts, almond paste, flour, and butter to a mixing bowl.
2. Mix at second speed for 2 minutes.
3. Add the egg whites and mix at second speed for 2 minutes till smooth.
4. Add the batter to a pastry bag with a star tip and "spritz" out 2-inch cookies onto a baking pan with baking paper.
5. Bake at 375°F (190°C) for 15 minutes.
6. Sprinkle a few sliced almonds on each cookie or leave plain.

Yields forty to forty-five ½ oz. (14 g) cookies on one baking tray

Almond Horn (Danish)

Nothing much beats a recipe that calls for just three ingredients yet turns out a chewy, sweet delight in twenty minutes that can be enjoyed by the whole family.

Also known as *Nøddehorn*, Almond Cloud Cookies, Almond Crescents, or *Mandelhörnchen*, Almond Horns are popular across Northern Europe and Scandinavia, although their precise origin is unclear.

Flourless, gluten- and dairy-free, with a taste a bit like marzipan, these little "horns" are wickedly dense, yet light, and can be made ahead of time. Thought to have been named in honor of a horned god who was celebrated at Winter Solstice in Nordic tradition, they are commonly served at Christmas and fill the windows of bakeries in Germany and Denmark especially. They are also popular in Italy, South Africa, and in Jewish culinary culture and are sold in most old-school Jewish delis in America.

Dip the ends in melted chocolate for extra sweetness, bake them with sliced almonds sprinkled on top for extra crunch, or eat them as they come. They can be stored in an airtight container in the fridge or frozen and defrosted later. You won't be disappointed as these cookies are guaranteed to be love at first bite.

INGREDIENTS:

- Almond paste—2 cups (441 g)
- Granulated sugar—1 cup (203 g)
- Egg white—1 (15 mL)

INSTRUCTIONS:

1. Add almond paste and sugar into a mixing bowl.
2. Mix at second speed for 5 minutes or until broken down to granulated pieces.
3. Add the egg white and mix for 3 minutes or until smooth.
4. Roll into 5-inch logs and twist into a horn shape. Place on a cookie sheet with baking paper.
5. Bake 400°F (200°C) for 20 minutes.

Yields eight 4 oz. (112 g) Almond Horns

Black and White Cookies
(American)

Manhattan is the spiritual home of the visually striking Black and White cookies, which were said to have first been created in the Bavarian-owned Glaser's Bake Shop in Yorkville. In fact, few pastries have a closer connection with New York than these.

More of a drop cake than a cookie, the idea to decorate these flattened mini cakes in half black and half white fondant icing with chocolate and vanilla flavoring was said to have been borrowed from a popular bakery called Hemstrought's in Utica, upstate New York.

Known there as "half-moon" cookies, another claim is that they date back to medieval times when the lunar cycle was revered. Modern-day thinking discounts that theory and suggests that they may simply have arisen out of the trend to have contrasting colors in baked goods.

These days, Black and Whites are sold all over America and are a popular staple in Jewish culture, making the top hundred of Jewish foods, perhaps for the nostalgia alone. But they are also made by Italian bakeries and Northern European bake shops. Children especially love them, and at Bea's we often see them breaking them in half and fastidiously eating one half before the other or nibbling carefully around the edges, often saving the chocolate to last.

For some, Black and Whites have come to represent racial harmony more than anything purely commercial or moon related. President Obama referred to them as "Unity Cookies" in one of his campaigns. As Lenny and Adaeze have a multi-racial marriage, they are especially relevant to Bea's Bakery and to the many happy multicultural customers we serve.

INGREDIENTS:

COOKIES:
- All-purpose flour—1¾ cups (222 g)
- Baking powder—½ teaspoon (2 g)
- Baking soda—¼ teaspoon (1 g)
- Table salt—¼ teaspoon (2 g)
- Sweet butter—10 Tablespoons (137 g)
- Granulated sugar—1 cup (203 g)
- Whole large egg—1 (45 mL)
- Vanilla extract—2 teaspoons (10 mL)
- Sour cream—⅓ cup (80 mL)

ICING:
- Sifted confectioners' sugar—5½ cups (1,068 g)
- Whole milk—7 Tablespoons (105 mL)
- Corn syrup—2 Tablespoons (30 mL)
- Vanilla—1 Tablespoon (15 mL)
- Salt—⅓ teaspoon (6 g)
- Cocoa powder—3 Tablespoons (25 g)

INSTRUCTIONS:

1. Whisk the flour, baking powder, baking soda, and salt together in a medium bowl. Set aside.
2. In a large bowl using a handheld or stand mixer fitted with a paddle attachment, beat the butter and sugar together on medium-high speed until smooth and creamy, about 2 minutes.

3. Add the egg and vanilla extract, and beat on high speed until combined, about 1 minute. Scrape down the sides and bottom of the bowl and beat again as needed to combine.

4. Reduce to low speed and add the dry ingredients in three additions, alternating with the sour cream. Beat everything on low until combined and no pockets of flour remain. The batter will be extremely thick.

5. Using a greased ¼-cup dry measuring cup, drop mounds of dough 4 inches apart on a baking pan with parchment paper, with six cookies per pan.

6. Bake at 350°F (180°C) for 20 to 25 minutes or until the edges are lightly browned. Allow cookies to cool on the baking pans for 5 minutes, then transfer to a wire rack to cool completely before icing.

7. Whisk the confectioners' sugar, 6 Tablespoons milk (90 mL), the corn syrup, vanilla extract, and salt together in a medium bowl. Transfer 1 cup of the icing to a separate bowl and add the remaining Tablespoon of milk and the cocoa powder. Whisk until combined.

8. Spread the vanilla icing onto half of the cookies on the flat side. Spread chocolate icing on the other side and allow the icing to set for a few minutes.

Yields twelve 3 oz. (84 g) cookies

Green & Whites
(Nigerian)

These colorful cookies are a link to my own ancestral home, as green and white are the colors of the Nigerian flag, chosen to represent Peace and Nature. They are eaten every year on the anniversary of Nigeria's independence. Made with pureed white yams, a staple of West Africa, they also have an age-old reputation for aiding fertility, especially the birth of twins.

This isn't just an old wives' tale. Central Africa has an unusually high rate of twins—with as many as forty-one twins being born for every thousand babies, when the norm is ten to fifteen. Producing a large family is considered to be a major accomplishment in our culture. My mother was a twin and so were many in my family, and she ate these "G&W" cookies throughout her pregnancy in the hope of producing her own. That didn't work out, but my brother and his wife recently had twins, so perhaps it had a longer-term effect.

Incredibly, a study by the Yale School of Medicine concluded that eating white yams at every meal, as many Africans do, might actually play a role in the higher incidence of twins. High in potassium, they also produce anti-estrogens that trick the body into producing more estrogen and increasing the rate of ovulation.

Every October, Nigerians the world over put on their traditional green and white "African lace" clothing to dance and eat handfuls of delectable G&Ws in celebration of their freedom from British rule. The richly embroidered fabric so favored by my people to denote status and wear for festivities came from longstanding links with the Austrian textile industry, but that's another story.

The good news is that, at Bea's Bakery, we sell these all year-round so anyone hoping for twins now has the perfect excuse to indulge.

Adaeze

INGREDIENTS:

COOKIES:
- Unbleached all-purpose flour—1¾ cups (222 g)
- Baking powder—½ teaspoon (2 g)
- Baking soda—¼ teaspoon (1 g)
- Table salt—¼ teaspoon (2 g)
- Sweet butter—10 Tablespoons (137 g)
- Granulated sugar—1 cup (203 g)
- Whole large egg—1 (45 mL)
- Vanilla extract—1 teaspoon (5 mL)
- Sour cream—⅓ cup (80 mL)
- Yams, mashed and pureed—¼ cup (60 mL)

ICING:
- Sifted confectioners' sugar—5½ cups (1,068 g)
- Whole milk—7 Tablespoons (105 mL)
- Corn syrup—2 Tablespoons (30 mL)
- Vanilla—1 Tablespoon (15 mL)
- Table salt—⅓ teaspoon (2 g)
- Green food dye—1 Tablespoon (15 mL)

INSTRUCTIONS:

Cookies:

1. Preheat the oven to 350°F (180°C).
2. In a medium bowl, whisk the flour, baking powder, baking soda, and salt together. Set aside.

3. In a large bowl, using a handheld or stand mixer fitted with a paddle attachment, beat the butter and sugar together on medium-high speed until smooth and creamy, about 2 minutes.
4. Add the egg and vanilla extract, and beat on high speed until combined, about 1 minute. Scrape down the sides and up the bottom of the bowl and beat again as needed to combine.
5. Reduce to low speed and add the dry ingredients, the sour cream, and the yams.
6. Beat everything on low until combined and no pockets of flour remain. The batter will be extremely thick.
7. Grease baking pans or line them with parchment paper.
8. Using a greased ¼-cup dry measuring cup, drop mounds of dough, 4 inches apart, on the prepared baking pans: six cookies per sheet.
9. Bake for 16 to 18 minutes or until the edges are lightly browned. The cookies will spread and be in a slight pyramid shape.
10. Allow the cookies to cool on the baking pans for 5 minutes, then transfer to a wire rack to cool completely before icing.

Icing:

1. In a medium bowl, whisk together the sugar, 6 Tablespoons of milk, the corn syrup, vanilla extract, and salt.
2. Transfer 1 cup (240 mL) of the icing to a separate bowl. Add the remaining Tablespoon of milk and the green food dye. Whisk until combined.
3. On the flat side of each cookie, spread the vanilla icing as a stripe in the middle. Spread green icing on each side. Allow the icing to set for a few minutes.

Yields twelve 3 oz. (84 g) cookies

Enjoy Green & White Cookies to celebrate Nigerian Independence Day or if you are a woman hoping to have twins.

Oatmeal Raisin Cookies
(American)

Although oatmeal cookies originated in England in the 1800s and were first brought to the United States by British settlers, the first American recipe appeared in 1896 from a Boston cook named Fannie Merritt Farmer.

After suffering a stroke as a teenager, Fannie was housebound but took up cooking for guests at her mother's boarding house. Self-taught, she trained until she was in her thirties and became so proficient that she was invited to take up the position of principal of the prestigious cookery school she'd attended. Within a decade, she had published her first cookbook, featuring almost two thousand recipes as well as advice on nutrition, culinary science, and housekeeping.

What started with a modest print run sold out time and again and became known as the *Fannie Farmer Cookbook* that is still in print today. So successful was Fannie that she set up her own eponymous cookery school and was invited to lecture at Harvard. Specializing in diets for the sick and convalescent—as she herself had been—she used a wheelchair in her final years and died at the age of fifty-seven after another stroke.

Her oatmeal raisin cookie recipe was initially created as an early kind of health food, as the cookies are low in fat and calories but high in iron and fiber and thought to lower cholesterol. They became so popular that the Quaker Mill Company of Ohio (which later became Quaker Oats) featured it on their iconic packs of oatmeal that we all know and love today. There is even a National Oatmeal Cookie Day each April, although—as our customers will testify—every day can be oatmeal raisin cookie day, as the taste of our sweet and crumbly treats is always a reason to celebrate.

INGREDIENTS:

- Unsalted butter—¾ cup (164 g)
- Margarine—¾ cup (173 g)
- Granulated sugar—¾ cup (152 g)
- Brown sugar—4 cups (893 g)
- Whole large eggs—4 (180 mL)
- Vanilla—4 teaspoons (20 mL)
- All-purpose flour—3 cups (381 g)
- Cinnamon—½ oz. (14 g)
- Salt—¼ oz. (7 g)
- Baking soda—½ oz. (14 g)
- Oats—4¼ cups (418 g)
- Raisins—2¼ cups (335 g)
- Water—½ cup (120 mL)

INSTRUCTIONS:

1. Add all ingredients to a mixing bowl.
2. Mix at second speed for 3 to 4 minutes until smooth.
3. Form 4 oz. balls of dough with your hands or a scoop and place on a sheet pan with baking paper.
4. Bake at 325°F (170°C) for 13 minutes.

Yields fifteen 4 oz. (112 g) cookies

Gluten-Free Version:

- Substitute the same amount of all-purpose flour with whole grain, gluten-free flour.

Mandelbrot

(Jewish)

Almond paste features in so many of our most popular items because it is such a great all-round ingredient that adds a distinctive taste as well as protein and goodness. Mandelbrot, a lighter, fluffier version of Italian biscotti, is so called because the Yiddish word for almonds is *mandl*.

Enjoyed by the Jews of Eastern Europe for two centuries since it originated in Germany, via Italy's Jewish population, mandelbrot is often prepared for the Sabbath and is especially popular among Ashkenazi Jews. Long-lasting and easy to make, these cookies take an hour to prepare and bake and are often twice cooked to extract the moisture. Our recipe calls for them to be baked for forty minutes and then toasted according to preference.

The Italian connection is key because the versatile almond paste first traveled there from the Far East and Arabia in the eleventh century BC. Almond trees are thought to have been the first domesticated variety of tree and can be dated back to the Bronze Age. There are two varieties—bitter and sweet—and early man had to be careful because the bitter variety contains toxins and must be roasted to be safe.

Fortunately, storebought almond paste is made of the sweet variety, and the tried and tested Bea's Bakery recipe for mandelbrot adds eggs, butter, salt, nuts, flour, and orange zest to give this delectable bite an even deeper, richer flavor. Shalom.

INGREDIENTS:

- Granulated sugar—2 cups (406 g)
- Salt—1 pinch
- Almond paste—5 oz. (140 g)
- Butter—4 oz. (112 g)
- All-purpose shortening—3½ oz. (98 g)
- Vanilla—1 teaspoon (5 mL)
- Orange zest—½ oz. (14 g)
- Whole large eggs—1½ (68 mL)
- Cake flour—3 cups (347 g)
- Baking powder—½ oz. (14 g)
- Granulated nuts (optional)—1 cup (120 g)

INSTRUCTIONS:

1. Add the sugar, salt, almond paste, butter, shortening, vanilla, and zest into a mixing bowl.
2. Mix at second speed for 2 minutes until smooth.
3. Add the eggs, cake flour, baking powder, and optional nuts and mix for 3 to 4 minutes or until the mix is smooth.
4. Roll out into 12 oz. logs and flatten on a baking pan with baking paper.
5. Bake at 325°F (170°C) for 40 minutes.
6. Cut into slices when cooled. Then turn over each slice and toast to desired color.

Yields four 12 oz. (336 g) Mandelbrot Logs

Coconut Macaroon
(Italian/Jewish)

Few languages are more poetic or romantic than that of Italy, and the Italian word *ammacare*—which means to crush—is the root of the more familiar word "macaron" or "macaroon."

Such is the beauty of language and of baking that what started in Venetian monasteries as a small almond-meringue cookie with a chewy center—sometimes called "priest's bellybuttons"—was introduced to French royalty before morphing into different variations as the rßecipe traveled.

The substitution of what would have been exotic shredded coconut instead of almond flour in the late 1800s by experimental chefs was a masterstroke and created a delicious new cousin of the original. The additional moisture also prevented the macaroons from spoiling during travel. When the original recipe changed yet again in Paris in the early 1900s to become a sandwich-style cookie with a buttercream filling, it became forever known as a macaron to distinguish it from the coconut variety.

Once coconut became more widely available and more affordable than almond powder, the sale of macaroons took off and became a regular feature of Jewish Passover celebrations. What were sometimes referred to as "coconut kisses" found their place on the Seder table originally because they contain no dairy and abide by religious dietary law. Before too long, major matzoh suppliers started selling premade coconut macaroons as a Passover treat.

At Bea's, these nostalgic bites never fail to sell out and we are only too happy to share our family recipe, which makes a mouthwatering ninety of the sweet kisses. Whether you make them for Passover or Christmas, Eid or Diwali, we know you'll love them. Enjoy!

INGREDIENTS:

- Egg whites—10 (150 mL)
- Granulated sugar—5½ oz. (154 g)
- Brown sugar—5½ oz. (154 g)
- Table salt—1 pinch
- Corn syrup—5 oz. (140 g)
- Shredded non-sweet coconut—40 oz. (1,120 g)
- Powdered sugar—20 oz. (560 g)
- All-purpose flour—5 oz. (140 g)
- Cornmeal—5 oz. (140 g)
- Vanilla extract—½ teaspoon (3 mL)

INSTRUCTIONS:

1. Add egg whites, granulated sugar, brown sugar, salt, and corn syrup to a pot over high heat till it comes to a full boil.
2. Let it sit for 5 minutes.
3. Add the egg white mixture and the remaining ingredients to a mixing bowl.
4. Mix at second speed for 2 minutes.
5. Add to a pastry bag and "spritz" small cookies onto a baking pan with baking paper.
6. Bake at 350°F (180°C) for 35 minutes.
7. Enjoy plain or dip in your preferred melted chocolate.

Yields ninety 1 oz. (28 g) macaroons

French Rolled Florentine
(French)

Florentines were originally made for Queen Catherine de' Medici of France by pastry chefs at the Palace of Versailles. They are delicate, lace-like cookies with caramel undertones and a chocolatey finish, and when they come out of a warm oven they are pliable enough to roll around a tube before they cool and dry into a crisp but chewy cylinder of deliciousness with a drizzled coating of melted dark chocolate. You can even fill them with buttercream for added richness if you like.

Perfect for dunking into coffee or a tiramisu dessert, rolled Florentines are so eye-catching that they are often given as gifts or made specially for Christmas. Catherine de' Medici, who was a true gastronome, liked them so much she was said to be delighted that they were named for her native city, although they may also have been named after the Florentine coins of the era.

Married to King Henry II of France, she was also the mother of a queen of Spain and not one but three consecutive French kings, two of whom died before she did. Catherine was a great patron of the arts. She is also credited with having introduced some of the fussier French dishes to Italian court, including Florentines.

With such a noble history, what's not to like about these elegant, regal little cookies? So put on your tiaras and start baking.

INGREDIENTS:

- Blanched almonds—4 cups (442 g)
- Unsalted butter—6 oz. (168 g)
- Granulated sugar—1½ cups (304 g)
- Corn syrup—½ cup (120 mL)
- All-purpose flour—1 cup (127 g)
- Heavy cream—½ cup (120 mL)
- Almond extract—2 teaspoons (10 mL)
- Vanilla extract—1 teaspoon (5 mL)
- Table salt—¼ teaspoon (2 g)
- Dark bittersweet chocolate—4 oz. (112 g)

INSTRUCTIONS:

1. Pulse almonds in a food processor until finely chopped.
2. In a medium saucepan, add the butter, sugar, and corn syrup, and heat over medium heat just until the butter is melted, stirring occasionally to blend. Do not boil the mixture.
3. Remove from the heat and add the chopped almonds, flour, cream, almond extract, vanilla, and salt. Stir to combine. Set the mixture aside to cool at room temperature for 20 minutes.
4. With a small cookie scoop, scoop six mounds of dough on a baking pan with parchment paper. Space them about 4 inches apart to allow for spreading. Bake at 350°F (180°C) until golden brown, about 10 minutes.
5. Allow the Florentines to cool on the cookie sheets for 3 minutes, then transfer them to a wire cooling rack.
6. When the cookies are completely cool, drizzle chocolate over the tops.

Rolled Florentine:

1. Follow the above instructions up to step 4.
2. Allow to cool on the baking pan for 2 minutes.
3. Use a thin-bladed spatula to remove the delicate cookies.

4. Shape them around a cigar tube, being careful not to burn your fingers as they are very hot.

5. Allow them to cool for 5 minutes. Then remove the tube and dip each end of the Florentine in melted chocolate.

Yields fifteen 4 oz. (112 g) Florentine rolls

Italian Cannoli

(Italian)

In Palermo, the capital of the Italian island of Sicily, the fried tubes of pastry known as cannoli were historically called *cappeli de Turchi* or Turkish hats—a nod to the ancient Arab Saracens who brought sugar to Italy and turned what was already a tasty treat into something truly sweet.

Later they became cannoli as a nod to the *canna* or reeds that were cut from the rivers and used as a mold around which to roll the pastry before frying. These days you can buy special cannoli tubes that do the job just as well.

This timeless dessert dates back centuries and is thought to have originated in Sicily, where they were made especially for the island's Carnivale, a celebration of food and drink in the cold, dark winter months before Lent. In a similar way to Mardi Gras, revelers take to the streets for days at a time—sometimes weeks—and are free to enjoy themselves without judgement.

The traditions vary up and down the country and can include masked balls as in Venice, extravagant floats and costumes, and even street fights with thousands of locally grown oranges. Whatever the celebration, cannoli are almost certain to feature. Although time-consuming and fiddly to make, generations of *nonnas* (grandmothers) have been rolling out little circles of pastry for years, before rolling them around a reed or frying them, and filling them with sweetened cream cheese.

Our creamy filling features ricotta cheese, vanilla, sugar, and chocolate chips to contrast with the crisp outer layer flavored with cinnamon and vanilla. You can switch out honey for sugar and add chopped nuts, pumpkin, and candied peel for variation. In Italy and around the world, they are eaten year-round, so we don't have to wait for Carnivale to enjoy them. *Deliziosa!*

INGREDIENTS:

SHELLS:

- All-purpose flour—3 cups (381 g)
- Granulated sugar—¼ cup (51 g)
- Cinnamon—¼ teaspoon
- Unsalted butter—3 Tablespoons (41 g)
- Vanilla—2 Tablespoons (30 mL)
- Room temperature water—2 Tablespoons (30 mL)
- Distilled white vinegar—1 Tablespoon (15 mL)
- Whole large egg—1 (45 mL)
- Egg yolk—1
- Egg white—1
- Frying vegetable oil—4 cups (950 mL)

EQUIPMENT:

- Cannoli tubes—6
- Pasta roller

FILLING:

- Ricotta cheese (whole milk)—2 cups (662 g)
- Powdered sugar—1 cup (203 g)
- Vanilla—1 splash
- Chocolate chips—2 oz. (56 g)

INSTRUCTIONS:

Shells:

1. Mix flour, sugar, and cinnamon together in a medium bowl. Cut in unsalted butter until crumbly.
2. Make a well in the center and add vanilla, water, vinegar, whole egg, and egg yolk.
3. Mix with a fork until the dough becomes stiff, then finish kneading it by hand on a clean surface (adding a bit more water if needed) for about 10 minutes. Cover with plastic wrap and refrigerate for 1 to 2 hours.
4. Divide cannoli dough into three balls; flatten each one to about ½-inch thickness.
5. Roll the first ball of dough through successively thinner settings on your pasta roller until you have reached the thinnest setting on your machine. Dust lightly with flour if necessary.
6. Place the sheet of dough on a lightly floured surface. Using a cutter or large glass, cut out 4- to 5-inch circles.
7. Dust the circles with a light coating of flour. This will help you later in removing the shells from the tubes. Roll dough around cannoli tubes and seal the edges with a bit of egg white. Repeat with the remaining dough balls.
8. Heat oil in a deep fryer or deep skillet to 375°F (190°C).
9. Fry shells on the tubes in hot oil, a few at a time, until golden, about 2 to 3 minutes. Use tongs to turn as needed. Remove the shells carefully using tongs, and place them on a cooling rack set over paper towels.
10. Cool just long enough that you can handle the tubes, then carefully twist the tube to remove the shell. Using a tea towel may help you get a better grip. Wash or wipe off the tubes and use them for more shells. Cooled shells can be placed in an airtight container and kept for up to 2 months. You should only fill them immediately or up to 1 hour before serving.

Filling:

1. Mix all ingredients in a bowl by hand or mixer. Do not overmix.
2. Fill a pastry bag with a round hole at the tip.
3. Fill each side of the cannoli shells and enjoy.

Yields six cannolis

Gingerbread Cookies

(Egyptian)

Honey-flavored gingerbread dates to Ancient Egypt and China, two places where ginger grows in abundance and honeybees created a product that never goes bad. In fact, honey was revered by the ancients for its taste and protein, plus its antibiotic and antiseptic qualities that promotes healing, especially with burns and other wounds.

The Egyptians had no idea that honey is also an antioxidant, helps prevent diabetes, and protects the heart, stomach, and nervous system from inflammation. They liked its taste and versatility, as well as the fact that all they had to do was plant some flowers and the bees would do the rest.

We can't promise that the 2½ cups of the magical syrup it takes to make a batch of these delicious cookies are going to be enough of a cure-all, but the result will certainly make you feel better. This is proven by the fact that the Egyptians and, later, the Greeks baked them for ceremonies and celebrations—as do we. The smell of gingerbread is still synonymous with the holidays.

The first known recipe dates to 2400 BC and was written down at a time when spices from the Far East were revolutionizing cooking in the West. After evolving from a soft, crumbly gingerbread that didn't keep very long, they morphed into a more portable and durable cookie that could be shaped into saints, animals, or plants depending on the event. It was the Germans in the sixteenth century who had the idea to make decorative "gingerbread houses" out of cookies that were traditionally much harder in Europe.

We can't guarantee that the delightfully doughy gingerbread cookies we make at Bea's would stand up to the task and, besides, they'd be gobbled up long before the builder completed the first wall!

INGREDIENTS:

- Brown sugar—2 cups (406 g)
- Butter—1 oz. (28 g)
- Whole large eggs—3 (135 mL)
- Whole milk—¼ cup (60 mL)
- Baking soda—2 Tablespoons (24 g)
- Table salt—1½ Tablespoons (29 g)
- Honey—2½ cups (600 mL)
- All-purpose flour—2½ cups (317 g)
- Rye flour—1¼ cups (129 g)
- Pastry flour—2½ cups (289 g)
- Molasses—2½ Tablespoons (38 mL)
- Ginger spice—¼ teaspoon
- Pumpkin spice—¼ teaspoon

INSTRUCTIONS:

1. Add all ingredients to a mixing bowl.
2. Mix at second speed for 8 to 10 minutes until smooth.
3. Sprinkle some all-purpose flour on a sheet pan, and then flatten the dough on top.
4. Refrigerate overnight.
5. Roll out the dough to ½-inch thick, and cut out desired shapes with 3-inch cookie cutters.
6. Place cookies on a cookie sheet with baking paper and bake at 275°F (140°C) for 18 minutes.

Yields twelve to eighteen 4 oz. (112 g) cookies

Almond Macaroon Cookies
(Italian)

Italy was a whole new experience for us on our recent ten-day visit there. We flew into Rome and enjoyed Milan, Florence, Venice, Siena, and San Giminiano, drinking in the culture and the food.

Wandering into their *pasticcerie* or pastry stores, our eyes lit up at the delicacies offered—row upon row of pretty little *pasticcini* topped with fruit and nuts, chocolate, frosting, and jelly. In the name of research, we felt it only fair to sample a few and we are happy to report that they didn't disappoint.

The Italians prop up the bars of their local cafés every morning and drink warm (not hot) cappuccino. They consider it a sacrilege to have one after ten o'clock. From then on, they only order *caffè*, a tiny strong shot of espresso, although they would rarely use that word. They also frown upon the way we vary and embellish our coffee, making frappuccini and lattes. In Italian, latte just means milk, so if you make the mistake of ordering one, that is what you'll get. Coffee is part of Italy's daily ritual, and they take it very seriously. Happily, they also love their sweet treats and almost always eat something small and light to go with it.

Knowing how many Italian clients we have at Bea's, we were inspired to take photos of some of the stunning displays and take notes for when we got home. We were also delighted to see that they all sold *ricciarelli*, the Italian almond cookies that we already serve an authentic version of in LA and which have long been a firm favorite.

Made from a simple blend of almond paste, egg whites, and sugar and topped with blanched almonds, the dense, slightly chewy cookie with a strong almond flavor is similar to a French macaron. We found it most often in Siena, a city that knocked us out with its sculptures, art, color, and beauty. Refreshed and inspired, we returned to California bursting with ideas, so watch this space. *Ciao!*

INGREDIENTS:

- Almond paste—2 cups (441 g)
- Powdered sugar—1 cup (194 g)
- Egg whites—5 (75 mL)
- Sliced blanched almonds—½ cup (55 g)

INSTRUCTIONS:

1. Add the almond paste and powdered sugar into a mixing bowl. Mix at second speed for 2 minutes.
2. Add 5 egg whites (60 mL), and mix for another minute or until the mixture is smooth.
3. Scoop the mixture into a pastry bag and squeeze out 2-inch, round cookies onto a cookie sheet with baking paper.
4. Sprinkle sliced almonds on top of each cookie.
5. Bake at 400°F (200°C) for 20 minutes until the cookies are lightly brown on the top.

Yields thirty 1 oz. (28 g) cookies

Enjoy Italian almond cookies as a special treat, for special occasions, or any day.

CHAPTER 4

Pies and Puddings

Fresh Fruit Tarte
(French)

*I*n medieval times, pies were considered suitable fare for common people, while open-topped tarts were for the nobility, who liked to see multiple layers of ingredients elegantly displayed. Early tarts or "quiches" were largely made with savory fillings including meat, fish, or vegetables, but those filled with custard, cream, and fruit were later variations that became even more popular.

This classic French-inspired *Tarte aux Fruits* is just that—a dense, fruit-filled crust packed with a rich combination of cream, sugar, and cream cheese. It makes a visually stunning and utterly delicious dessert, especially in the summer, and never fails to delight.

We love to use a mix of red and blue summer berries with additional splashes of sunshine and color provided by vibrant slices of mango and kiwi. You can be as creative as you like, and layer the fruit neatly in concentric circles, pile them into chunky segments, or make a geometric pattern that Albert Einstein would be proud of. And feel free to try different fruits like peaches, apricots, grapes, or cherries.

As the French would say, *Vive la difference!*

INGREDIENTS:

CRUST:

- All-purpose flour—1 cup (127 g)
- Granulated sugar—3 Tablespoons (13 g)
- Table salt—1 pinch
- Heavy cream—⅓ cup (80 mL)
- Unsalted sweet butter—6 Tablespoons (27 g)
- Whole large egg—1 (45 mL)
- Room temperature water—4 teaspoons (20 mL)

FILLING:

- Cream cheese—⅓ cup (73 g)
- Sour cream—½ cup (120 mL)
- Powdered sugar—½ cup (101 g)
- Vanilla extract—2 teaspoons (10 mL)
- Table salt—1 pinch
- Heavy cream—⅓ cup (80 mL)

TOPPINGS:

- Blueberries—½ cup (79 g)
- Strawberry halves—½ cup (79 g)
- Raspberries—½ cup (79 g)
- Kiwi halves—½ cup (79 g)
- Mango slices—½ cup (79 g)
- Clear jell paste—2 Tablespoons (30 mL)

INSTRUCTIONS:

1. Add the all-purpose flour, granulated sugar, table salt, heavy cream, unsalted sweet butter, whole large egg, and room temperature water into a mixing bowl.
2. Mix for 5 minutes at second speed till dough is all one piece.
3. On a lightly floured surface, roll the dough into an 11-inch circle. Transfer the crust to a 9-inch, round fluted baking tart pan with a removable bottom. Press the crust into the pan and trim the edges right at the top of the tart pan sides. (Do not worry if the crust cracks! Patch it up with the dough pieces that were trimmed from the edges.) Prick the bottom of the crust all over with a fork. Place the tart pan in the freezer for 30 minutes.
4. During the last 20 minutes of chilling, preheat the oven to 400°F (200°C). Prick the crust all over with a fork. Bake for 12 to 14 minutes, until the crust is golden brown. Transfer to a wire rack and cool to room temperature.
5. In the bowl of an electric mixer fitted with a whisk attachment, beat the cream cheese, sour cream, powdered sugar, vanilla extract, and salt on medium speed until smooth and creamy, 2 to 3 minutes. With the mixer on medium-low speed, gradually pour in the heavy cream and beat until the mixture is light and fluffy, about 30 seconds. Pour the cream cheese mixture into the crust and spread in an even layer.
6. Arrange the blueberries, strawberries, raspberries, kiwi, and mango on top of the filling. Microwave the jell paste in a small microwavable bowl until melted and smooth, about 30 seconds. Brush the jell over the fruit. Chill the tart until it is cold and the filling is set, at least 2 hours or overnight.

Yields one 9-inch tart

Bea's Classic Pumpkin Pie
(American)

Pumpkin pie feels so quintessentially American, and it is true that it is rarely eaten anywhere beyond our shores. The earliest versions are thought to date back to the Plymouth settlers in New England in the seventeenth century, when pumpkins cultivated by the Native American tribes were shared with the newcomers. Hence they featured prominently in the first ever Thanksgiving harvest supper, and every year since.

Pumpkins are closely related to melons, and their name comes from the Greek *pepon* for melon, which was changed variously to *pompoen* and then *pumpion* over time. Easy to grow from seed, they store well and have multiple uses, as well as making makeshift bowls once hollowed out. The settlers initially copied the Natives by cutting off the top of the fruit, removing the seeds, and filling it with honey, a little fresh milk, and whatever spices they had to hand before placing it in hot ashes to cook. In time, the resulting pudding was scooped out and used for cakes and as a tart filling.

It was a French chef, not an American one, however, who first published a recipe for a Pumpkin Torte in a pastry case in the seventeenth century. His pumpkin custard filling featured salt, sugar, and flaked almonds. "Pumpion pie" began to surface in English cookbooks soon afterwards, with added ingredients including fresh apple and dried fruit, as well as spices such as cloves, nutmeg, and cinnamon.

The first American recipe for "pumpkin pudding" appeared in 1796 in Connecticut from Amelia Simmons, who called herself "an American orphan" and was thought to have been a domestic cook. Her book had the not-so-catchy title of: *American Cookery, or the art of dressing viands, fish, poultry, and vegetables, and the best modes of making pastes, puffs, pies, tarts, puddings, custards, and preserves, and all kinds of cakes, from the imperial plum to plain cake: Adapted to this country, and all grades of life.*

She had all bases covered, and so do we with a simple recipe that takes less than an hour to make and bake and features pumpkin filling, sugar, eggs, and evaporated milk that can be poured into a prebaked pie crust. Happy Thanksgiving!

INGREDIENTS:

- 8-inch prebaked pie crusts—3
- Canned pumpkin (any brand)—24 oz. (672 g)
- Brown sugar—12 oz. (336 g)
- Corn starch—1 oz. (28 g)
- Salt—1 pinch
- Whole large eggs—4 (180 mL)
- Evaporated milk—24 oz. (672 g)
- Cinnamon—2½ oz. (70 g)

INSTRUCTIONS:

1. Refer to the crust instructions in the Fresh Fruit Tarte recipe on page 174 and bake for 8 to 10 minutes until light brown.
2. Add all ingredients (except the crusts) to a mixing bowl.
3. Mix with a wire whisk till smooth.
4. Pour mix into 8-inch pie tins with prebaked pie crusts to the top of the pie tins.
5. Bake at 375°F (190°C) for 35 minutes.

Yields three 8-inch pies

Lemon Meringue Pie
(American)

This timeless dessert takes us back to an era when American diners had revolving glass display cases illuminated from within on which the owners would proudly present a magnificent lemon meringue pie alongside a yummy cheesecake, a platter of chocolate éclairs, and a selection of deliciously decadent cakes.

At Bea's, we still have the bakery's original display case, and—yes—lemon meringue is a guaranteed showstopper there, lighting up the eyes of children and grandparents alike. For many, it's like going back to a time of mom-and-pop stores, drive-in theaters, iconic twenty-foot-long cars, bobby socks, and soda shops.

Like many great culinary creations, the lemon meringue pie is thought to have been born out of necessity and invention, when Elizabeth Goodfellow, the principal of a Philadelphia cookery school came up with a lemon custard pie that was so rich it called for ten egg yolks. Faced with the dilemma of what to do with all those spare egg whites, the resourceful Mrs. Goodfellow decided to whip them with sugar and add a meringue topping to her famous lemon pie.

It was one of her students who took it further and published the recipe in her cookbook in 1847, adding that a meringue improves any baked pudding. Variously called lemon cream pie, or iced lemon pie, the fancy lemon meringue concoction became a favorite treat of President Lincoln and was soon a Southern staple, by which time it had three distinct layers—a flaky pastry crust, the creamy lemony filling, and meringue as soft as a pillow.

Of all the pies we serve, this one has to be one of our bestsellers and—better still—it's a personal favorite of Lenny and Adaeze too. So remember, when life gives you lemons…make lemon meringue pie.

INGREDIENTS:

CRUST:
- Prebaked 9-inch pie crust—1

FILLING:
- Granulated sugar—1 cup (203 g)
- All-purpose flour—2 Tablespoons (16 g)
- Cornstarch—3 Tablespoons (36 g)
- Salt—¼ teaspoon (2 g)
- Room temperature water—1½ cups (360 mL)
- Lemon zest—from 2 lemons (10 g)
- Lemon juice—¼ cup (60 mL)
- Sweet butter—2 Tablespoons (27 g)
- Egg yolks—4 (60 mL)

MERINGUE:
- Egg whites—4 (60 mL)
- Granulated sugar—1 cup (203 g)

INSTRUCTIONS:

1. Refer to the crust instructions in the Fresh Fruit Tarte recipe on page 174 and bake for 8 to 10 minutes until light brown.
2. Preheat the oven to 325°F (170°C) and prebake the crust for 20 minutes.
3. To make the filling, whisk sugar, flour, cornstarch, and salt together in a medium saucepan; stir in water, lemon juice, and lemon zest. Cook over medium-high heat, stirring frequently, until the mixture comes to a boil. Stir in butter.
4. Place the egg yolks in a small bowl and gradually whisk in ½ cup of the hot sugar mixture. Then, whisk the egg yolk mixture back into the remaining sugar mixture. Bring to a boil and continue to cook while stirring constantly until thick. Remove from heat and pour the filling into the baked pastry shell.
5. To make the meringue, beat the egg whites in a glass, metal, or ceramic bowl until foamy. Gradually add sugar, continuing to beat until stiff peaks form. Spread meringue over the pie filling, sealing the edges at the crust.
6. Bake at 375°F (190°C) for 25 minutes till golden brown.

Yields one 9-inch pie

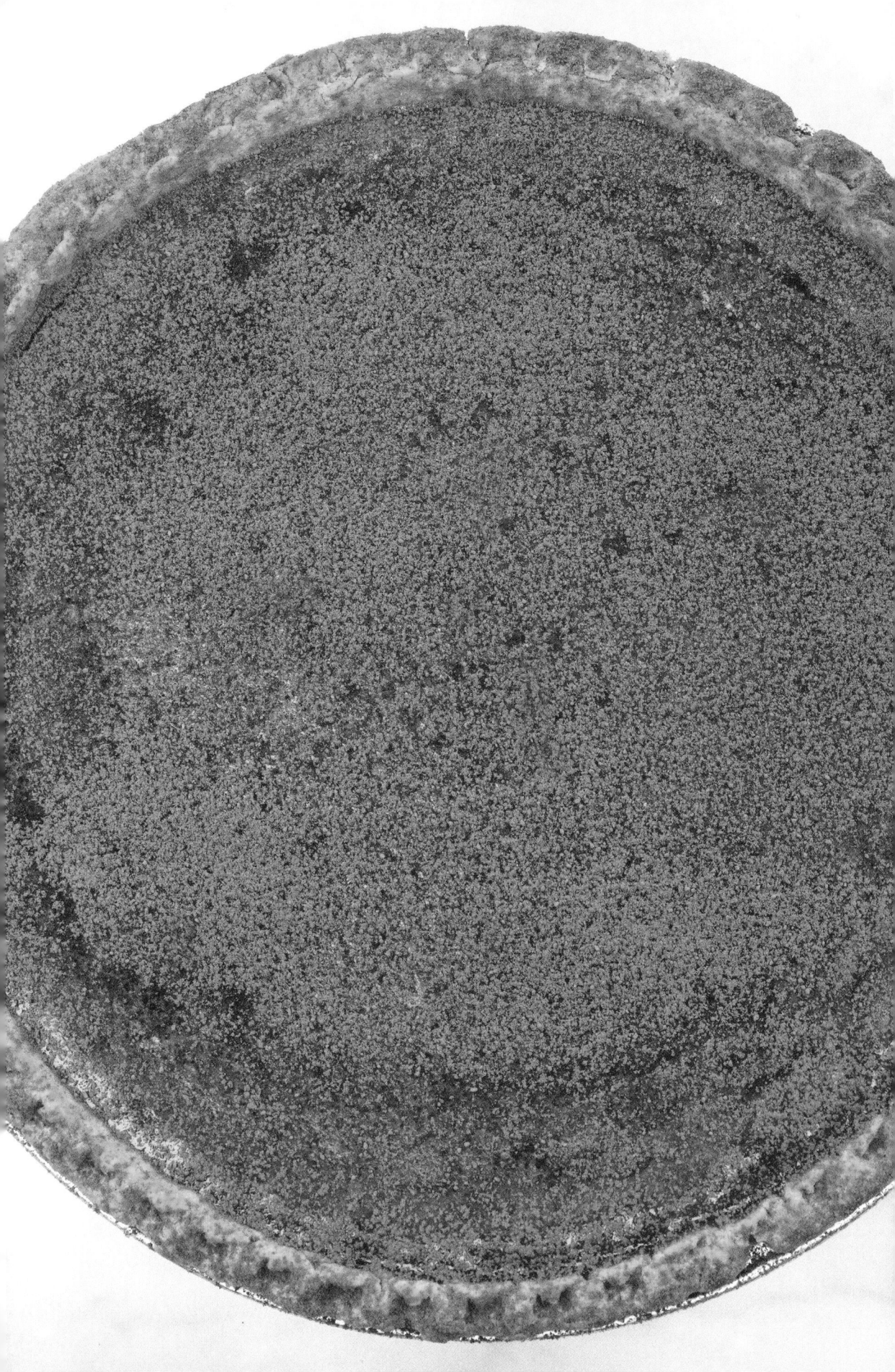

Adaeze's Southern Sweet Potato Pie (Southern)

Talking of personal favorites, this heirloom pie featured throughout Adaeze's childhood in the South where it has been enjoyed for generations. A classic of the Southern states, its creamy texture is similar to pumpkin pie, but it's not so distinctively flavored with spices that it can only be eaten at Thanksgiving.

Easy to make ahead of time and perfect for a family dinner, especially in the fall, the pie is a delicious centerpiece for the table that relies on a few simple ingredients—baked sweet potatoes, butter, sugar, eggs vanilla, and evaporated milk—all mashed together to make a light, fluffy filling that's scooped into a prebaked pie crust.

Like pumpkins, cooking sweet potatoes dates to the food that Native Americans ate, as they relied on fruit and vegetables grown locally. Also sometimes known as yams, even though they are very different from African yams, the tubers of these vine plants hail from South America originally and are related to the Morning Glory plant so loved by gardeners. They prefer tropical warmth and moisture but are otherwise relatively easy to grow and contain good levels of beta-carotene and vitamin A. Most sweet potatoes sold globally come from China and the rest from Africa, but North Carolina provides 60 percent of the US consumption.

A key component of what is known as "soul food," the ethnic cuisine of African Americans, sweet potatoes formed a vital part of the diet of African slaves who made dishes with any ingredients they could find that were like those they remembered from home. Choosing the sweet potato as a good substitute for yams, the enslaved West African cooks added them to dishes like gumbo and fried chicken, black-eyed peas, cornbread, and collard greens.

Hundreds of years of food culture have passed since then, with every kind of fusion, but the sweet potato has survived as a reliable and tasty member of the soul food family. This dessert pays homage to its longevity and versatility. Manna from heaven, it truly is a glory.

INGREDIENTS:

- Sweet potatoes—3
- Sweet butter—½ cup (109 g)
- Granulated sugar—1 cup (203 g)
- Vanilla—2 teaspoons (10 mL)
- Evaporated milk—½ cup (120 mL)
- Whole large eggs—2 (90 mL)
- 9-inch prebaked pie crust—1

INSTRUCTIONS:

Prepare the Crust:

1. Refer to the crust instructions in the Fresh Fruit Tarte recipe on page 174 and bake for 8 to 10 minutes until light brown.

Bake the Sweet Potatoes:

1. Preheat the oven to 400°F (200°C). Scrub the sweet potatoes until clean and prick them four to five times with a fork.
2. Place onto a baking pan and bake for 45 to 50 minutes, until the sweet potatoes are tender when pricked with a toothpick.
3. Remove from the oven and allow to cool until they can easily be handled. Peel off the skins, and place the sweet potatoes into a large mixing bowl. Reduce the oven heat to 350°F (180°C).

Make the Pie Filling:

1. Add butter to the sweet potatoes and mash until smooth. Add the sugar to the sweet potatoes and mix until well combined.
2. Add the vanilla extract, milk, and eggs and mix until well combined. Pour the filling into the unbaked pie crust.
3. Bake the pie until the center of the pie is set or about 1 hour. Remove the pie from the oven and allow to cool slightly.

Yields one 9-inch pie

Lenny's Famous New York Apple Pie (American/English)

This iconic dish seems to sum up the American spirit—big, bold, and full of flavor. To use a well-known phrase, it is "as American as apple pie." No Fourth of July barbecue would be complete without one, and an apple pie often accompanies the traditional pumpkin pie at Thanksgiving feasts.

What's a little surprising is that apple trees from Asia weren't even introduced to North America until the Pilgrims set sail from Europe in the fifteenth century with cuttings and seeds. And, naturally, the English in particular brought their favorite fruit recipes with them, of which cider and apple pie were the top two. Interestingly, the apples were originally cooked in a solid pastry case known as a "coffin" to contain it, with the shell discarded after serving. It was only when the Dutch arrived in the fifteenth century that an attractive and edible pie crust was introduced.

It was another three centuries before the recipe appeared in any American cookbook, by which time spices from the Far East were added to enhance the flavor. And by the twentieth century, it was so closely connected with our country's culture that American soldiers fighting the war in Europe often said they were "fighting for mom and apple pie."

Strongly associated with maternal love, home, and comfort, apple pie is the type of comfort food that always makes people smile. We see that all the time at Bea's and the look of delight on their faces when they get a first taste of Lenny's family recipe. He uses Granny Smith apples (which hold their shape best when baked), butter, flour, sugar, and cinnamon. He then rolls out the pastry and cuts it into strips to make a pretty lattice pattern on the top of the steeped fruit. Not only does this make the pie look more attractive to the eye, but as the apple filling cooks it rises up through the gaps to provide a mouthwatering aroma that can only be satisfied by eating a big thick slice. God bless America for taking in this versatile immigrant fruit and making it our own.

INGREDIENTS:

FILLING:
- Sweet butter—8 teaspoons (36 g)
- All-purpose flour—3 Tablespoons (24 g)
- Room temperature water—¼ cup (60 mL)
- Granulated sugar—1 cup (203 g)
- Granny Smith apples—6 to 7 apples or 7 cups sliced (907 g)
- Cinnamon—1½ teaspoons (4 g)

ASSEMBLING THE PIE:
- Premade pie crusts—2
- Whole large egg—1 (45 mL)
- Water—1 Tablespoon (15 mL)

INSTRUCTIONS:

1. Melt the butter in a pan over medium heat. Stir in 3 Tablespoons flour (24 g) then simmer for 1 minute, whisking constantly. Whisk in the water and sugar, then bring to a boil. Reduce heat and continue simmering for 3 minutes, whisking frequently, then remove from heat.

2. Peel, remove cores, and thinly slice 7 cups of apples (907 g) and place them in a large bowl. Sprinkle with the cinnamon and toss to combine. Pour the sauce over the apples and stir to coat.

3. Refer to the crust instructions in the Fresh Fruit Tarte recipe on page 174. Do not prebake the pie crust.

4. Sprinkle your work surface with flour and roll out the first pie crust to a 12-inch diameter circle. Wrap it around your rolling pin to transfer it to a 9-inch pie plate. Add the apple mixture to the pie plate, mounding slightly in the center and being careful not to get the filling on the edges, which would make it difficult to seal.

5. Roll the second crust into an 11-inch round and cut into ten even thickness strips using a wheel knife. Arrange the strips in a woven lattice pattern over the top. Beat together the egg and water and brush the top with the egg mixture.

6. Bake at 425°F (220°C) in the center of the oven for 15 minutes. Reduce the heat to 350°F (180°C) and continue baking another 45 minutes or until the apples are soft and the filling is coming up through crust.

Yields one 9-inch pie

Chocolate Mousse Pudding
(French)

You've probably all heard of the French post-Impressionist painter Henri Toulouse-Lautrec, who was famous for painting Parisian café society, circus performers, and can-can dancers at the Moulin Rouge, but did you know that he is also credited with inventing chocolate mousse?

The man, who stood at only 1.4 meters because of a bone disease, died of his hedonistic lifestyle at the age of thirty-six, but produced many iconic artworks that chronicled the social history of the time. He was also a talented chef, creating his own signature dishes and dangerously toxic cocktails for friends every Friday night. These inventive and often strange dishes included grilled grasshoppers, pike from the Somme, thrushes in juniper, and a heron roasted over an open fire. They were published in a book called *The Art of Cuisine* after his death.

He may have been a master with the paintbrush and an experimental genius in the kitchen, but his mastery of language wasn't quite so good because he named his famous dessert *mayonnaise de chocolat*. Thankfully it was later changed to *mousse de chocolat*, as "mousse" means foam. There is some debate whether he created or adapted the recipe, but we love to imagine that creative Frenchman standing over a bowl, whipping cream into a blend of sugar and eggs before pouring in bittersweet dark chocolate.

That's what we call art.

INGREDIENTS:

- Whole large eggs—3 (135 mL)
- Granulated sugar—4 oz. (112 g)
- Heavy cream—3 cups (710 mL)
- Melted dark bittersweet chocolate—4½ oz. (126 mL)

INSTRUCTIONS:

1. In a pot over medium heat, stir the eggs and sugar till they are warm to the touch.
2. Transfer the egg and sugar mixture to a mixer and whip at second speed for 3 to 4 minutes.
3. Add the heavy cream to the whipped eggs and sugar, and whip at second speed for 5 minutes or until the mix fluffs up in the bowl.
4. Then add the melted chocolate quickly, so it does not lump up. Whip at third speed or until the mix is a nice chocolate color.
5. Pour into chilled serving dishes.

Yields six 4 oz. (112 g) dishes

English Bread Pudding
(English)

Recycling and "upcycling" are words that have become very familiar to those of us born in this modern world, as we look to find ways to reduce waste and put anything surplus or leftover to good use.

Well, English cooks as far back as the eleventh century were doing their own bit for the environment when they decided to "recycle" leftover stale bread and turn it into this deliciously comforting pudding. To begin with, they simply soaked hard bread in water and then pressed it into a dish before adding sugar and spices before baking. Sometimes known as "poor man's pudding" because of its cheapness and simplicity, there is nothing poor about its flavor or its ability to fill hungry mouths.

Not surprisingly, the popularity of this humble dessert has seen it exported all over the world, with many regional variations depending on the type of bread used. It first arrived in America with the settlers and quickly spread around the globe, where cooks began to soak the bread in milk, eggs, and some sort of fat, giving rise to the name "bread and butter pudding."

Countries from the Philippines to Panama and Cuba to Canada have their own ways of transforming stale bread into something sweet and special, adding anything from fresh fruit to maple syrup, coconut to cream cheese, whisky to rum. Our version used stale challah bread, which makes it deliciously buttery and light; it's made with heavy black bread in Germany, with lighter-than-air *panetonne* in Italy, they use milk bread in Belgium, it's puff pastry in Egypt, and rusks are used in parts of the Middle East.

The beauty of this versatile dish is that it can be made with whatever you fancy or have leftover in your kitchen. So, go ahead and upcycle something you might otherwise have thrown away or fed to the birds. You know it makes sense.

INGREDIENTS:

- Challah bread—½ lb. loaf (75 g)
- Whole large eggs—4 (180 mL)
- Granulated sugar—¼ cup (51 g)
- Whole milk—1 cup (240 mL)
- Heavy cream—1 cup (240 mL)
- Cinnamon—½ Tablespoon (4 g)
- Vanilla extract—1 Tablespoon (15 mL)

INSTRUCTIONS:

1. Slice up challah bread into cubes.
2. Add the bread cubes and the remaining ingredients into a bowl and mix by hand for 1 minute.
3. Add to an 8-inch baking pan.
4. Bake at 325°F (170°C) for 40 minutes.

Yields one 8-inch pan

CHAPTER 5

Muffins and Scones

New England Bran Muffin
(American)

The origin of the word "muffin" has long been a subject of debate and may come from the Low German word *muffen* meaning small cake, or from the French *mou-pain* for soft bread. Either way, this cupcake-sized, bready delight has become an American tradition that has been teasing taste buds all over the world since the eighteenth century.

Served as an individual portion in a perfect, bite-sized round, the fresh muffins rise to a pleasing peak while the older, "quick bread" variety cooked on a griddle are flatter and are referred to as English muffins. The ones we are most familiar with are moist, rich, and usually sweetened, although there are several savory varieties that have also become very popular, such as cheese and vegetable (including sweetcorn, onions, and zucchini).

The New England bran muffins are so called because cooks from that region seemed to prefer a higher amount of bran and molasses than those from other areas. Wheat bran, a byproduct of milling, was originally added as an aid to digestion because of its high fiber and nutritional content and appeared in early cookbooks for invalids. Used to enrich bread and breakfast cereals, it became more widely used and was adopted for biscuits and cookies as well as muffins.

The first known recipe for bran muffins was published in Philadelphia in 1857, but others quickly followed, and the New England moniker stuck, giving these treats a wholesome, nostalgic feel that stirs up memories of home cooking and checked tablecloths. At Bea's, our bran muffins with raisins, buttermilk, eggs, and orange peel are fluffy, moist, and perfect for any time of day, but especially breakfast. Enjoy!

INGREDIENTS:

- Wheat bran—2¼ cups (302 g)
- Buttermilk—1½ cups (360 mL)
- Vegetable oil—¾ cup (180 mL)
- Whole large eggs—1½ (68 mL)
- Brown sugar—1 cup (223 g)
- Orange peel—½ oz. (14 g)
- All-purpose flour—¾ cup (95 g)
- Whole wheat flour—¼ cup (29 g)
- Table salt—1 pinch
- Baking soda—1 Tablespoon (12 g)
- Baking powder—½ Tablespoon (6 g)
- Black raisins—¾ cup (135 g)

INSTRUCTIONS:

1. Add wheat bran and buttermilk to a mixing bowl.
2. Mix at second speed for 2 minutes and scrape down the bowl with a plastic scraper.
3. Add the rest of all ingredients to the bowl and mix at second speed for 3 minutes.
4. Scrape down mixing bowl, then mix at second speed for another minute.
5. Using baking pan spray, spray a 12-cup baking pan and fill all 12 holders with baking cups.
6. Using spoons or an ice cream scoop, dish 4 oz. (112 g) of batter into each baking cup.
7. Bake at 325°F (170°C) for 25 minutes.

Yields twelve 4 oz. (112 g) muffins

Blueberry Muffins
(American)

Did you know that blueberries have been grown in North America for something like 13,000 years? These delicious natives to our shores were enjoyed by the earliest inhabitants for their flavor, versatility, and health benefits. Related to cranberries, huckleberries, and bilberries, they were used as medicine, for dyeing cloth, and to add vitamins and sweetness to food.

Growing wild in wooded areas where they could be picked at will, they weren't cultivated commercially until 1916, when they were tamed and developed into "highbush" varieties in New Jersey (as opposed to the wild "lowbush" type). These days, American farmers produce 40 percent of the world's supply of highbush berries, which amounts to one billion pounds of blue fruit every year. The humble blueberry has become so much a part of our history that only it and the cherished strawberry have their own emojis on our smartphones.

As we are all much more focused on the health benefits of food these days, you'll be delighted to know that the blueberry is heart-healthy and high in antioxidants and vitamins and recommended for everything from brain and heart health to helping with diabetes and stomach problems.

These yummy little berries are now readily available fresh or frozen, powdered, canned, pureed, or liquified. Blueberries go great with bananas and citrus flavors and are the must-have ingredient for a great cheesecake as well as blueberry pie, jam, and muffins. At Bea's, our muffin recipe has the added delight of a sweet crumb topping made of brown sugar, butter, flour, and cinnamon to add a delicious flourish to what was already a bestseller in our bakery. It's almost too good to eat.

INGREDIENTS:

- All-purpose flour—1½ cups (190 g)
- Granulated sugar—¾ cup (152 g)
- Baking powder—2 teaspoons (8 g)
- Salt—½ teaspoon (3 g)
- Extra virgin olive oil—⅓ cup (80 mL)
- Whole large egg—1 (45 mL)
- Whole milk—⅓ cup (80 mL)
- Organic blueberries—1 cup (158 g)

INSTRUCTIONS:

1. Whisk the flour, sugar, baking powder, and salt together in a large bowl.
2. Pour the olive oil into a liquid measuring cup. Add the egg and enough milk to reach the 1-cup mark; stir until combined. Pour into the flour mixture and mix just until the batter is combined. Fold in the blueberries and set the batter aside.
3. Scoop 4 oz. of batter per cupcake (or about three quarters full) into a cupcake tray prepped with muffin cups. Bake in the preheated oven at 400°F (200°C) for 25 minutes or until a toothpick inserted in the center of a muffin comes out clean.

Yields twelve 4 oz. (112 g) muffins

Double Chocolate Muffin
(American)

Having first appeared in print in 1703 as *moofin*, the word has since become synonymous with home baking and comfort eating. In Britain in the Victorian era, "muffin men" did a roaring trade of selling freshly baked muffins, crumpets, and buns to hard-working folk who only had Sundays off and little time to do their own baking. The children's song, "The Muffin Man" dates to a nursery rhyme of those times, when traders wandered the streets of London with trays of baked goods balanced on their heads crying out their wares.

Nowadays, we have very few such street vendors because food is available to us in so many other ways, not least by cooking it ourselves at home. These mouthwatering chocolate delights are made in the traditional way of American muffin-making by adding the moist ingredients of yogurt, eggs, milk, olive oil, and vanilla into the dry ingredients of flour, sugar, chocolate chips, and cocoa powder before baking for twenty minutes or until perfectly done.

With twelve muffins per batch, there will be plenty to go 'round, and these crowd-pleasers might even inspire a singalong: "Do you know the Muffin Man, the Muffin Man, the Muffin Man? Have you seen the Muffin Man, who lives in Drury Lane?"

INGREDIENTS:

- All-purpose flour—2 cups (254 g)
- Granulated sugar—1 cup (203 g)
- Cocoa powder—½ cup (67 g)
- Baking soda—1 teaspoon (3 g)
- Dark bittersweet chocolate chips—1 cup (302 g)
- Plain yogurt—1 cup (240 mL)
- Whole milk—½ cup (120 mL)
- Extra virgin olive oil—½ cup (120 mL)
- Whole large egg—1 (45 mL)
- Vanilla extract—1 teaspoon (5 mL)

INSTRUCTIONS:

1. Combine the flour, sugar, cocoa powder, baking soda, and ¾ of the chocolate chips in a large bowl.
2. Whisk the yogurt, milk, oil, egg, and vanilla in separate bowl until smooth.
3. Pour the yogurt mixture into the chocolate mixture and stir until the batter is just blended.
4. Scoop 4 oz. of batter per cupcake (or about three quarters full) into a cupcake tray prepped with muffin cups. Then sprinkle with the remaining ¼ of the chocolate chips.
5. Bake at 350°F (180°C) for 20 minutes or until a toothpick inserted in the center of a muffin comes out clean. Cool in the pans for 10 minutes before removing to cool completely on a wire rack.

Yields twelve 3 oz. (84 g) muffins

Kichel—with a Sugar-Free Version (Jewish)

Whenever my father came home from the bakery, he always made sure to bring a bag of fresh kichel for my mother, Clara, who ate them every night after dunking them in her coffee. Born in Poland, at ninety-four years old she still so loves what are sometimes known as "Jewish bow tie cookies" that we regularly ship a supply to her home in New Jersey.

The name of these tasty little treats comes from the Yiddish for cookie or "little cake" and has its roots in the Ashkenazi Jewish culture of Eastern Europe. Made from flour, sugar, and eggs, the dough is rolled out thinly and then twisted into little bow ties.

Light and airy, these "nothing" puff pastries are eaten by the bagful and are traditionally consumed during the Friday night blessing and at Rosh Hashanah or Jewish New Year, when they are served with pickled herring and schnapps. The best kichels are paper thin, crispy on the outside but soft inside, and melt in your mouth. Some people fry theirs, but we prefer to bake ours so that there is no trace of grease.

For many people, kichels are a nostalgic reminder of family Shabbat meals, mom-and-pop bakeries, and the golden age of Jewish baking. At Bea's, which was established in the 1960s, these little cookies sum up what it means to be the last full-service homemade Jewish-style bakery in Los Angeles.

Just ask my mom.

Lenny

INGREDIENTS:

- Granulated sugar—1 oz. (28 g)
- Table salt—1 pinch
- Whole large eggs—4 (180 mL)
- Extra virgin olive oil—½ cup (120 mL)
- All-purpose flour—1 cup (127 g)

INSTRUCTIONS:

1. Add the sugar, salt, eggs, olive oil, and flour in a mixing bowl. Mix at third speed for 7 to 8 minutes or until the dough comes off the sides of the bowl cleanly.
2. On a floured surface, roll out the dough so it's flat. Using a knife, cut the dough into small rectangles of about 2 x 4 inches.
3. Then, twist each rectangle and place on a baking pan with parchment paper; each piece should be an inch apart.
4. Bake at 375°F (190°C) for 30 minutes.
5. Then bake at 390°F (200°C) for about 10 minutes or until they are a light brown color.
6. If needed, lower to 350°F (180°C) for another 10 minutes to finish cooking. You do not want them to dry out.

For a Sugar-Free Version:

- Substitute monk fruit sugar for the granulated or omit the sugar altogether.

Yields twenty 2 oz. (56 g) kichel

Enjoy Kichel with coffee.

British Buttermilk Scones
(English)

Scones are a traditional British bakery item, similar to American biscuits, that are thought to have originated in Scotland in the sixteenth century. No one is sure where the name came from, although the Oxford English Dictionary claims it may be a mutation of the Dutch and German *schoonbrot* or *sconbrot*, meaning fine bread.

How to pronounce the word opens a whole new and often controversial debate, although saying "skon" or "skone" are both widely accepted. However you say it, scones were first made with oats and griddled over an open fire, but were later shaped out of dough made from flour, sugar, sour milk (or buttermilk), and eggs and baked in an oven. This creates a crusty shell that breaks open to reveal crumbly softness inside. Variations include the addition of cheese, dried fruit, and even nuts and chocolate in some bakeries, although the Brits would almost certainly frown upon that.

While we in America tend to eat them plain and on their own, the custom in Britain is as sacrosanct as their traditional afternoon tea. Often forming the centerpiece of the table along with finger sandwiches, cookies, and a pot of hot tea, scones are sliced in two and slathered in butter. They are then smeared with strawberry jam and a large dollop of clotted cream. Believe it or not, there is another entire and often divisive debate about whether the jam or the cream should come first.

With more than five hundred years of history, these venerable treats deserve the respect they have earned over the centuries, and our British friends and customers love that we make them at Bea's. One relative who lives in London insists on having a scone for breakfast every day, and friends in New York stock up on our scones whenever they come to California. So, make yourself a batch and settle down to a proper British tea. Cheers!

INGREDIENTS:

- All-purpose flour—5 cups (635 g)
- Granulated sugar—1 cup (203 g)
- Sweet butter—2 cups (437 g)
- Baking powder—1 Tablespoon (12 g)
- Baking soda—1 teaspoon (4 g)
- Table salt—1 pinch
- Buttermilk—1½ cups (360 mL)
- Whole large eggs—3 (135 mL)
- Vanilla—1 teaspoon (5 mL)

INSTRUCTIONS:

1. Add flour, sugar, sweet butter, baking powder, baking soda, and salt to a mixing bowl and mix at second speed for 2 minutes.
2. Add the buttermilk, eggs, and vanilla and mix at second speed for 2 minutes.
3. Separate the dough into pieces that are 4 oz. each (use scale to weigh).
4. Place on a baking pan with parchment paper.
5. Bake for 35 minutes at 350°F (180°C) or until the scones are lightly brown on top.

Yields ten 4 oz. (112 g) scones

Oat Currant Scones
(Scottish)

This tasty regional variation of English buttermilk scones has a fascinating history which began when the Romans first imported oats to conquered Great Britain to feed their horses in the first century AD.

The healthy crop fared especially well in Scotland, thanks to its rainfall and longer daylight hours, and before too long those enslaved by the Romans began to cook the abundant grain in water or milk. This made a porridge—from the Old English word "pottage," a thickened soup—that could be eaten warm for breakfast or sliced up when cold and eaten at night to feed hungry mouths.

This nutritious and savory baked cookie is thought to have been the world's first ever type of "fast food," as it could be eaten on the move and helped fueling the country's armies with energy.

Oats, and porridge in particular, soon became so synonymous with Scotland that they have maintained a place in the nation's heart ever since. These oatmeal scones with eggs, heavy cream, currants, walnuts, and vanilla are a perfect way to combine the Scottish love of both the organic crop dating back centuries and the scone that originated in that country more than five hundred years ago (see British Buttermilk Scones on page 219). *Slàinte!*

INGREDIENTS:

- All-purpose flour—2½ cups (317 g)
- Granulated sugar—½ cup (101 g)
- Baking powder—1¼ Tablespoons (15 g)
- Cream of tartar—½ teaspoon (6 g)
- Salt—1 pinch
- Unsalted butter—6 oz. (168 g)
- Rolled oats—1½ cups (148 g)
- Heavy cream—1 cup (240 mL)
- Whole large eggs—3 (135 mL)
- Vanilla—4 Tablespoons (60 mL)
- Currants—¾ cup (119 g)
- Walnuts—¾ cup (90 g)

INSTRUCTIONS:

1. Add all ingredients to a mixing bowl and mix at second speed until smooth.
2. Separate the dough into pieces that are 4 oz. each.
3. Place on a baking pan with parchment paper.
4. Bake at 350°F (180°C) for 30 minutes.

Yields ten 4 oz. (112 g) scones

Gluten-Free Version:

- Substitute the same amount of all-purpose flour for whole grain, gluten-free flour.

CHAPTER 6

Specialty Sweet Breads

Chocolate Babka
(Polish)

This rich and decadent fresh yeasty loaf with ribbons of gooey chocolate running through it is traditionally served at Easter or other holiday occasions when all bets are off when it comes to watching what you eat.

It's a recipe that requires time and patience as you must wait for the dough to rise, but it is well worth the effort. The name *babka* derives from the Slavic word *babcia* which means "little grandmother" in Polish and Ukrainian. This treat is thought to have originated in the Jewish communities of Eastern Europe. To begin with, it was relatively plain and was comprised of leftover challah bread, nuts, and spices, but then cooks made their own buttery dough and added fruit, cheese, almond paste, poppy seeds, and spices. Once chocolate became more readily available in the twentieth century, it was added to make it sweeter.

By the time babka traveled to Israel with early settlers, it became known as fresh yeast cake, and when it arrived in New York, it became especially popular with Ashkenazi Jews, who claimed it as their own. These days, all nationalities and creeds can enjoy the half-bread, half-cake delight at Bea's, where it makes a perfect snack to have with tea or coffee and is delicious at any time of the year.

INGREDIENTS:

- Fresh yeast—2 oz. (56 g)
- Whole milk—1 cup (240 mL)
- Water—1 cup (240 mL)
- Orange flavor (orange peel)—½ oz. (14 g)
- All-purpose flour—4 cups (508 g)
- Unsalted butter—1 cup (219 g)
- Granulated sugar—½ cup (101 g)
- Table salt—¼ oz. (7 g)
- Whole large eggs—6 (270 mL)
- Melted unsalted butter—½ cup (109 g)
- Melted bittersweet chocolate—1 cup (240 mL)
- Chocolate cake crumbs—1 cup (168 g)
- Bittersweet mini chocolate chips—1 cup (302 g)
- Granulated sugar mixed with a pinch of cinnamon—½ cup (203 g)

INSTRUCTIONS:

1. Pour fresh yeast, milk, water, orange peel, and half the flour into a mixing bowl.
2. Mix for 2 minutes till all combined.
3. Dust flour over the top of the dough.
4. Let sit for 45 minutes till the dough comes up and breaks through the flour dusting.
5. Add the butter, sugar, salt, eggs, and the remaining flour to the mixing bowl.

6. Mix at second speed for 10 minutes or until the dough separates cleanly from the mixing bowl.
7. Separate the dough into six 14 oz. pieces. Then roll them flat.
8. Brush with melted butter and add the melted chocolate, chocolate crumbs, chocolate chips, and cinnamon sugar. Roll up and twist into loaf baking pans with baking paper.
9. Cover with plastic wrap and let proof for 2 hours.
10. Bake at 350°F (180°C) for 45 minutes.

Yields six 14 oz. (392 g) babkas

Irish Soda Bread
(Irish)

In these days of multiple food intolerances, Irish soda bread has inadvertently become much loved by those who can't tolerate fresh yeast. And with its basic ingredients of flour and salt, combined with the magic mixture of baking soda and buttermilk which makes it rise, it is also one of the quickest and easiest breads to make. What's not to like?

Aside from its cleaner qualities, soda bread has devoted followers the world over for its unique texture and taste that places it high on the comfort food list. It was once served at almost every meal in Ireland, since the leavening agent "bread soda" was first introduced just before the Irish Potato Famine in the early nineteenth century. Soda bread was born out of necessity—like so many recipes.

Using milk that had gone off or the sour liquid left over from making cheese and butter, Irish cooks quickly discovered that the buttermilk and soda combined to create the same effect as fresh yeast, allowing the dough to rise enough to make a perfect round. A cross was almost always cut in the top of the risen dough, "to ward off the devil" according to folklore—the true purpose was to allow the bread to cook evenly.

At Bea's we make the American version of Irish soda bread which adds sugar, raisins, and eggs to give it more the texture of a scone or cake. Some recipes also add caraway seeds, and the loaf has become especially popular among our customers with Irish ancestry and on St Patrick's Day. We always advise our customers that this is a bread that doesn't keep, but that doesn't seem to be a problem. Once sliced and slathered in butter and jam, or dunked in a steaming pot of Irish stew, the temptation to keep going and have another slice or two means that it doesn't need to.

INGREDIENTS:

BREAD:
- All-purpose flour—2½ cups (317 g)
- Granulated sugar—½ cup (101 g)
- Salt—½ teaspoon (3 g)
- Baking soda—½ teaspoon (2 g)
- Butter—4 oz. (112 g)
- Buttermilk—¾ cup (180 mL)
- Whole large eggs—2 (90 mL)
- Black raisins—1 cup (158 g)

TOPPINGS:
- Whole large eggs—2 (90 mL)
- Water—½ cup (120 mL)

INSTRUCTIONS:

1. Add all ingredients to a mixing bowl.
2. Mix at second speed for 5 minutes until all ingredients are combined and smooth. The dough should be a bit sticky to the touch.
3. Separate the dough into 1 lb. (450 g) loaves.
4. Roll each into a ball and flatten on a sheet pan with baking paper.
5. Cut a cross with a knife on top of the dough.
6. Mix large whole eggs and water together to make egg wash.
7. Brush with egg wash for shine.
8. Bake at 325°F (170°C) for 40 minutes.

Yields three 1 lb. (450 g) loaves

Nigerian Cornbread
(Nigerian)

Cornbread is one of those age-old recipes that feels like it's been around forever as a quick comfort food. Made from yellow cornmeal ground from corn maize that had been dried or roasted, like so many recipes it has its origins in the cuisine of the Native Americans, who gave it names like *nokechick* and *apan*.

When Europeans first landed on American soil, they soon fell for the tasty and nutritious food that quite literally saved them from starvation during the earliest, harshest years of colonization. To begin with, it was nothing more than a porridge-like "hominy" mixed with water and heated over a fire. This later became known as "grits" after the Old English *gryts*, meaning coarse meal.

Once they started to make bread from the cornmeal, people discovered that it traveled well, so when the Europeans headed out to be pioneers, they made loaves of "journey cake"—a description that later evolved into "Johnny cake."

After cultivated corn was introduced to West Africa during the dark days of the slave trade, cornbread was also adopted there, and it was something that Adaeze knew and loved as a child from her Nigerian family. It was also favored by the slaves in the Southern states, where it became a vital staple of their diet.

By the eighteenth century, the taste for variations led to the addition of other ingredients as they became available. Eggs, buttermilk, and baking soda made it more palatable, as did the addition of meat, cheese, and vegetables. Sweeteners such as sugar or honey weren't added until the twentieth century.

The delicious cornbread we make at Bea's has the added touch of smoked paprika and basil to make it authentically Nigerian, and we also throw in the kernels from a fresh cut cob to give it some bite. Baking one of America's oldest known foods has never been easier and this forty-minute recipe proves it.

INGREDIENTS:

- All-purpose flour—1 cup (127 g)
- Cornmeal—1 cup (173 g)
- Granulated sugar—½ cup (101 g)
- Salt—½ teaspoon (3 g)
- Baking powder—2 teaspoons (8 g)
- Smoked paprika—½ teaspoon (4 g)
- Basil—½ teaspoon (1 g)
- Fresh corn on the cob—1 (287 g)
- Whole large eggs—2 (90 mL)
- Melted sweet butter—½ cup (109 g)
- Whole milk—1 cup (240 mL)

INSTRUCTIONS:

1. Add all the dry ingredients to a mixing bowl (flour, cornmeal, sugar, salt, baking powder, paprika, and basil) and mix at first speed for 2 minutes.
2. Cut the kernels off the ear of corn.
3. Add the eggs, butter, milk, and corn kernels to a pot over medium heat until warm.
4. Pour the warm egg mixture into the mixer with the dry ingredients and mix for 2 minutes.
5. Pour the batter into one 8-inch round baking pan with baking paper.
6. Bake for 30 minutes at 350°F (180°C). Check when done with a toothpick in the middle. If it's not done, put back in the oven for a few minutes and test again.

Yields one 8-inch baking tin

CHAPTER 7

More Sweet Treats

Apple Noodle Kugel
(Jewish)

When I was a little girl, I used to be taken to an Éclairs bakery in New York every weekend by my German godfather to eat his favorite apple noodle kugel. I had no idea that the chain was once owned by the father of my future husband, Lenny. I just knew that the food there was the greatest.

My godfather David Weber had become my mentor when I was a young woman studying design in Manhattan. He had an incredible family history; his ancestors arrived in America on the *Mayflower*, and he could trace his family back generations. A vivacious personality who worked for CNN, he taught me so much about culture and the arts, as well as instilling in me some of his German pride. Within a short time, he became like a second father to me and, when I introduced him to my parents, they adored him as much as I did and made him my unofficial godfather. Now almost eighty, he has even moved to LA to be closer to me.

Every time I eat apple noodle kugel, I think of David and our time in Éclairs talking about everything from cultural differences to politics and history. Although I knew nothing of Jewish traditions and food, I was interested to learn that kugel has a long history dating back to medieval times when noodles were first introduced to Europe by Asian traders. Called *lokshen* in Yiddish, the noodles were often made out of leftover bread pastry and baked into sweet and savory cakes with sugar, cream, and eggs. They soon became a staple of the Ashkenazi diet in particular. For sweet varieties, any fruit was used, including plums, cherries, and apricots, but apple and soaked raisins became the most popular.

Children and people new to this tasty treat often refer to it as "pasta cake," and in a way that's exactly what it is, but once they've had their first mouthful, they are instant fans, just as I was. *Mazel tov!*

Adaeze

INGREDIENTS:

- Wide egg noodles, cooked—2 cups (360 g)
- Apple, diced—½ (43 g)
- Whole large eggs—8 (360 mL)
- Half & half cream—2 cups (480 mL)
- Granulated sugar—1 cup (203 g)
- Baking powder—½ Tablespoon (6 g)
- Cinnamon—½ Tablespoon (4 g)

INSTRUCTIONS:

1. Add all ingredients to a mixing bowl and mix until all ingredients are combined.
2. Pour batter into 8-inch square baking tins. Bake for 45 minutes at 300°F (150°C).

Yields two 8-inch baking tins

Matzo Kugel
(German / Jewish)

No Jewish kitchen would be without a box of matzo: the crunchy, unleavened flatbreads that play such an integral role in the ceremonial Seder meal that heralds the start of Passover week. Often referred to as "the bread of affliction," intended to remind us of our humility, humble matzo is eaten to commemorate the end of the Israelites' enslavement and their hasty exodus from Egypt.

Without any specific flavor, this dry crisp bread that has a long shelf life is a versatile base for many recipes. It can be ground into cakes or fashioned into balls for matzo ball soup, soaked and then fried like French toast, switched in for pizza dough or sheets of lasagna, or used to great effect in this kugel recipe.

Perhaps the most famous matzo producer in America was the Manischewitz brand, a factory that made kosher products founded by an enterprising rabbi in Ohio in 1888. Now the world's largest producer of matzo, making almost a million matzos per day, it revolutionized the production of the holy unleavened bread by introducing machines that cut and baked the product in accordance with strict religious rules.

This easy-peasy kugel recipe calls for seven sheets of the square matzo that Rabbi Manischewitz would instantly recognize, along with eggs, cream, raisins, sugar, almonds, cinnamon, and vanilla. It can be eaten all year-round by everyone, but for our Jewish customers we wish them *Sameach Pesach*! Happy Passover.

INGREDIENTS:

- Standard square matzo—7 sheets (210 g)
- Black raisins—½ cup (79 g)
- Whole large eggs—6 (270 mL)
- Half & half cream—1 cup (240 mL)
- Vanilla extract—1 teaspoon (5 mL)
- Granulated sugar—1 cup (203 g)
- Sliced blanched almonds—½ cup (55 g)
- Cinnamon—1 pinch
- Baking powder—½ teaspoon (2 g)

INSTRUCTIONS:

1. Crush the matzo into small, penny-sized pieces in a bowl.
2. Pour the rest of the ingredients into the bowl and mix up by hand.
3. Grease two 8-inch baking pans.
4. Pour mix into both pans and bake at 300°F (150°C) for 45 to 50 minutes till golden brown on top.

Yields two 8-inch pans

Nigerian Egg Rolls
(Nigerian)

Anyone who has ever been to Nigeria will be familiar with these delicious, hard-boiled eggs wrapped in a spicy, sweet batter before being fried, as they are sold on almost every street corner by enterprising sellers.

Inspired by the meaty Scotch eggs so beloved of Brits, these beloved oval snacks are a little fiddly to make but well worth the effort. The trick is to not overcrowd the pan and to keep the temperature to a medium heat to make the perfect batter shell. When the balls look brown on one side, flip them over to make them evenly brown.

First brought to Nigeria and Cameroon by British colonists, the Nigerians soon added their own unique flavors in keeping with their tastes and made it a more affordable bite by replacing the traditional pork sausage and breadcrumb coating with batter.

Flaky and crunchy on the outside, the dough gives way to a soft, protein-rich egg to make the perfect breakfast treat or convenient party appetizer. In Nigeria, the hugely popular egg rolls are traditionally served warm and dipped in a hot chili pepper sauce, but these can be eaten on their own, with ketchup, or any sauce you fancy. Have fun!

INGREDIENTS:

- Lukewarm water—½ cup (120 mL)
- Fresh yeast—1 teaspoon (5 g)
- All-purpose flour, plus extra for dusting—3 cups (381 g)
- Granulated sugar—3 teaspoons (13 g) (or more)
- Nutmeg—1 teaspoon (3 g)
- Salt—1 teaspoon (6 g)
- Paprika—1½ teaspoons (4 g)
- White pepper—½ teaspoon (8 g)
- Unsalted butter—4 Tablespoons (55 g)
- Whole milk—⅔ cup (160 mL)
- Hard-boiled eggs, shells removed—6 (109 g)

INSTRUCTIONS:

1. In a small bowl, add the warm water, fresh yeast, and a sprinkle of sugar and set aside for about 5 minutes until it foams.
2. In another bowl, sift together all the dry ingredients: flour, sugar, nutmeg, salt, paprika, and white pepper.
3. Cut the butter into pieces and add the butter to the dry ingredients and mix all together.
4. Add the fresh yeast mixture and the milk. Mix thoroughly to incorporate all the ingredients, but don't overwork the dough. If the dough sticks to your palm, you can sprinkle in a Tablespoon of flour at a time to get a soft but not sticky dough.
5. Cut the dough into quarters or halves and place on a floured work surface.
6. Roll the dough to about ¼-inch thickness and use a dough cutter or any round object to cut the dough into a 5-x-5-inch square piece of pastry.

7. Place a hard-boiled egg in the dough you cut out and pinch and/or roll on your palm to close the opening of the dough to form a ball. Make sure you don't make any holes in the dough while doing this.
8. Place the dough ball on a floured surface (you can use a baking pan) and gently place the closed end facedown.
9. Repeat the process with the remaining dough. When you are done, cover the dough balls with plastic wrap and let the dough rest for about 30 minutes.
10. In a large saucepan or a fryer, add vegetable oil and heat to about 350°F (180°C).
11. Drop the dough balls gently into the hot oil and fry for about 4 to 5 minutes or until golden brown. Flip the dough over and fry the other side until golden brown.
12. Remove egg rolls from the oil and drain on a paper towel. Repeat the frying process until you finish all the dough.

Serve warm with your favorite drink. Enjoy!

Yields six egg rolls

Éclair
(French)

When my father expanded from his original Peter Pan bakery to what became a quite famous chain of bakeries in New York, he named his stores Éclairs after the favorite pastry treats known around the world for two centuries. With sweet happenstance, Adaeze used to go to a branch with friends and family when she was younger so, although my dad no longer ran them, there was a connection between us long before we met.

Chocolate éclairs were a sure-fire bestseller in his stores, and it's not at all surprising. What's not to like? An easy to eat oblong of light choux pastry filled with vanilla-flavored pastry cream and smothered in chocolate icing, it checks all the boxes for those with a sweet tooth.

Created in Lyon, France, in the nineteenth century, allegedly by Napoleon's baker Antonin Carême, the name éclair means "flash of lightning" as they are very often devoured in a flash. Originally called *pain à la Duchesse* (Duchess bread or little Duchess), Carême—who also cooked for the Romanovs of Russia—added the glaze to make them even more delicious. They are so revered in France that there is a National Éclair Day and every so often there is a competition for the pastry chef who can make the longest. The current world record held by a Belgian is 503 meters.

The éclairs we sell at Bea's are far more manageable, at ten centimeters long. They are just like the ones I used to eat in my father's bakery. At Bea's, we have several French customers including one who comes in just for our éclairs, and cries, "Take me home!" each time he is given his box of delights. They take him straight back to his happy childhood in France, eaten "in a flash" with his morning coffee. *Bon Appetit!*

INGREDIENTS:

PASTRY DOUGH:
- Water—2 cups (480 mL)
- Shortening—1 cup (221 g)
- High gluten flour—1½ cups (190 g)
- Baking powder—1½ teaspoons (6 g)
- Whole large eggs—6 (270 mL)
- Whole milk—½ cup (120 mL)

PASTRY CREAM:
- Whole milk—2 cups (480 mL)
- Granulated sugar—4 oz. (112 g)
- Cornstarch—3 Tablespoons (36 g)
- Egg yolks—2 (90 mL)
- Whole egg—½ (23 mL)
- Unsalted butter, cubed—4 Tablespoons (55 g)
- Vanilla extract—½ Tablespoon (8 mL)

CHOCOLATE ICING:
- Powdered sugar, sifted—5½ cups (1,068 g)
- Corn syrup—2 Tablespoons (30 mL)
- Vanilla—1 Tablespoon (15 mL)
- Table salt—⅓ teaspoon (2 mL)
- Whole milk—7 Tablespoons (105 mL)
- Cocoa powder—3 Tablespoons (25 g)

INSTRUCTIONS:

Pastry Dough:
1. Preheat the oven to 325°F (170°C).
2. Combine the water and shortening in a medium saucepan and bring it to a boil.
3. Transfer to a mixing bowl. Add the flour, baking powder, eggs, and milk.
4. Mix at second speed (cream) for 5 minutes.
5. Put the mixture into a pastry bag. You can also use a sandwich bag and cut a small hole at the bottom.
6. On a baking pan, greased or lined with parchment paper, "spritz" out dough, so each éclair is shaped into a 4-inch tube.
7. Bake for 45 minutes or until golden brown.

Pastry Cream:
1. In a medium saucepan, bring milk and 2 oz. (56 g) of sugar to a simmer over medium-high heat. Whisk constantly to avoid burning.
2. In a heatproof bowl, combine the egg, egg yolks, cornstarch, and remaining 2 oz. (56 g) of sugar. Whisk to combine.
3. Add a quarter of your hot milk mixture to the egg mixture *very* slowly, while whisking constantly to temper your egg yolk mixture. Whisk until smooth.
4. Slowly add the rest of the milk, whisking constantly. Return mixture to the saucepan and bring to a simmer.
5. Once your mixture starts bubbling, reduce the heat to medium and continue whisking for 2 to 3 minutes to ensure the mixture is cooked and properly thickened.
6. Pour your mixture into a heatproof container and place your butter cubes on top, allowing them to melt. Do not cover.
7. Allow your pastry cream to cool until just warm to the touch. Stir in your butter and then add in the vanilla extract.
8. Cover with plastic wrap so that it's touching the surface of the pastry cream to avoid a skin forming. Put in the refrigerator to cool; you can keep in the fridge for 2 to 3 days.

9. When the cream is cooled, take a spatula and scoop it into a standard pastry bag with a ¼-inch tube or ¼-inch hole cut in the tip of the pastry bag.
10. Make holes in both ends of the éclair with any ¼-inch stick, then squeeze pastry cream from the bag into the éclair at both ends till it is filled.

Icing:

1. In a medium bowl, whisk the confectioners' sugar, corn syrup, vanilla extract, salt, and 6 Tablespoons of the milk together.
2. In the same bowl, add the remaining Tablespoon of milk and the cocoa powder. Whisk until combined. With a knife, spread a layer of icing on each éclair.

Yields eighteen 4-inch éclairs

Enjoy a chocolate éclair with your morning coffee, for an afternoon break, or anytime you need a special treat.

Danish Pastries
(Danish)

Legend has it that these delicious pastries, that millions of us enjoy with our morning coffee, first got their name for an unusual reason—an industrial strike. When workers in Danish bakeries staged a walkout over pay and conditions in 1850, the owners brought in foreigners to replace them and were impressed by the pastries they made. The traditional creations of the Austrian bakers were especially popular, including their *Plundergebäck*—mini tarts of the lightest puff pastry with a sweet custard filling.

Although they were new to Danes, the Austrians had been making these flaky pastries with gooey fillings for hundreds of years, ever since the recipe traveled from the Arab Moors in Spain to the rest of Europe. One myth claims that a French chef originally invented this lighter-than-air pastry by mistake when he forgot to add butter to his pastry dough. He was said to have folded butter into the mix at the last minute to come up with a technique called lamination that we know and love to this day. This has since been thrown into doubt by the discovery of a thirteenth century recipe from a Moorish cookbook that has a similar technique.

Wherever it originated, it was the Austrians who took it to Denmark, and when the Danish bakers eventually returned to work, they adopted the delectably airy treat and adapted it in all sorts of different ways, adding fresh or dried fruit, alcohol, nuts such as almonds or hazelnuts, poppy seeds, spices such as cinnamon or cardamon, and frosting or toppings of caramel, sweet jam, or lemon curd. It soon became a stalwart of Scandinavian food culture known there as *Wienerbrød*—or Vienna bread—while the rest of the world called it simply Danish.

Our recipe couldn't be simpler and takes less than an hour to prepare. We add cinnamon sugar but leave it open for you to then add whatever topping your heart desires. So, channel your inner Dane and pay homage to hard-working bakers everywhere.

Poy-poy! (Good luck)

INGREDIENTS:

- Active fresh yeast—1 oz. (28 g)
- Granulated sugar—¼ cup (51 g)
- Table salt—3 oz. (84 g)
- All-purpose shortening—1 cup (221 g)
- Patent flour—¾ cup (99 g)
- Room temperature water—½ cup (120 mL)
- Whole large eggs—2 (90 mL)

INSTRUCTIONS:

1. Add all ingredients to a mixing bowl and mix for 5 minutes or until smooth.
2. Roll out dough on a floured surface to about ½-inch thick.
3. Spread your favorite fruit filling evenly over the dough.
4. Sprinkle cinnamon sugar on top if desired.
5. Cut into 2-inch wide strips.
6. Roll up into wheels at about 4 oz. (112 g) each.
7. Lay flat on baking pan with the wheels facing up.
8. Add your desired fruit toppings and then bake at 325°F (170°C) for 40 minutes.

Yields eight 4 oz. (112 g) Danishes

Butter Streusel
(German)

One thing you might try sprinkling on top of your Danish pastry is streusel, a crumbly topping of sugar, butter, and flour similar to that you'd use to finish off a fruit crumble. Streusel originated in Germany and comes from the word of the same name that means to sprinkle, strew, or scatter.

There are very few treats that couldn't benefit from a bit of streusel on top, including muffins, pies, cakes, breads like babka, and puddings. It can also be added as a crumbly ribbon layer for additional texture and is a vital ingredient in German crumb cake or *Streuselkuchen*, piled as high as the baker chooses.

As well as the three key ingredients (in which the sugar is always dominant), we add cinnamon and vanilla to our streusel, but any combination of spices, chopped nuts, or even oats can be added, depending on taste.

Mix in a food processor or by hand until you have a course, clumpy crumble. The beauty of this topping is that you can make a batch and then, once sealed in a bag or container, it will store for months, ready to be added to anything you fancy baking. The possibilities are endless.

INGREDIENTS:

- Granulated sugar—1 cup (203 g)
- Sweet butter—1 cup (219 g)
- Pastry flour—2 cups (264 g)
- Vanilla—½ teaspoon (3 mL)
- Salt—1 pinch
- Cinnamon—2 oz. (56 g)

INSTRUCTIONS:

1. Add all ingredients to a mixing bowl and mix at second speed for 2 minutes.
2. Crumble on top of your favorite buns or muffins before you bake them.

Yields enough crumb toppings for a 12-x-12-inch cake

Brownies
(American)

Everyone likes to be associated with a success story and the chocolate brownie is just such a tale. So, the question of whether a Maine housewife accidentally forgot to add baking powder to her chocolate cake in the late 1800s or if a Chicago socialite had her chefs create something easy and portable for boxed lunches around the same time remains largely unanswered.

The Maine connection came from several cookbooks that published recipes for "Bangor brownies," citing the state's lumber port on the Penobscot River. The city's mystery housewife who is said to have omitted the baking powder was never named, but her delicious mistake lives on.

Another legend credits its creation to chefs at a Chicago hotel who were asked by the owner's wife to make a packable dessert for boxed lunches to give to female guests visiting the Chicago World Fair in 1893. They came up with a chocolate brownie finished with an apricot glaze, which sounds a bit sticky and risky for ladies in their finery.

Whoever first came up with the idea of a dense square of chocolatey delight, it is such a staple of American life that we even have a National Brownie Committee, and it estimates that we consume between 1.5 and 4 billion of them every year. That's a lot of brownies!

Our recipe is nut-free, but fans of the sticky treat are fiercely divided on whether they should contain walnuts, pecans, or be just as we make them—pure and sweet. The beauty of the brownie is that you can add whatever you like, and many varieties don't even feature chocolate but are flavored instead with vanilla (known as blondies), caramel, peanut butter, coconut, or marshmallow.

Whatever your choice, the most difficult part will be deciding how long the pan of brownies will last. The national average is one to two days, but Southerners claim an entire baking tray of brownies can be consumed in less than two hours. Enjoy!

INGREDIENTS:

- Granulated sugar—1½ cups (304 g)
- All-purpose flour—¾ cup (95 g)
- Cocoa powder, sifted—⅔ cup (45 g)
- Powdered sugar—½ cup (98 g)
- Dark chocolate chips—½ cup (151 g)
- Sea salt—¾ teaspoon (5 g)
- Whole large eggs—2 (90 mL)
- Extra virgin olive oil—½ cup (120 mL)
- Water—2 Tablespoons (30 mL)
- Vanilla—½ teaspoon (3 mL)

INSTRUCTIONS:

1. Add the sugar, flour, cocoa powder, powdered sugar, chocolate chips, and salt to a mixing bowl and mix at second speed for 1 minute.
2. Add the eggs, olive oil, water, and vanilla, then mix at first speed until the batter is smooth.
3. Pour the batter into an 8-x-15-inch baking pan with baking paper and smooth the top. Bake at 325°F (170°C) for 45 minutes.

Yields one 8-x-15-inch baking tray

Gluten-Free Version:

⋄ Substitute the same amount of all-purpose flour for whole grain, gluten-free flour.

Rum Balls
(Danish)

Bakers are extremely resourceful and always willing to adapt recipes or fashion something out of their mistakes. They are also great at using up leftovers, and these delicious rum balls evolved from exactly that.

When bakeries in Denmark closed at the end of the day and there were unsold cakes, cookies, and pastries sitting on the shelves not fresh enough to sell the following day, some clever bakers decided to do something with the treats that might otherwise be thrown away.

Breaking them up and beating them into crumbs, they mixed them with honey or syrup, rum, sugar, cocoa powder, and nuts to make these truffle-like delicacies that are now enjoyed the world over. Other variations include the addition of dried fruit, jam, condensed milk, and even whole cherries. Once rolled into roughly the size of a golf ball or smaller, the rum balls don't even need to be cooked and can be coated in anything from sprinkles to desiccated coconut, chopped nuts to powdered sugar.

They are especially popular in Europe at Christmas, but in the Southern United States they are often known as bourbon balls, after the liquor they prefer to add. In Denmark, rum balls are known variously as *romkugle*, *sputnik*, or *truffle* and often come covered in brightly colored sprinkles of every hue. And, in 2017, Danish schoolchildren helped create the world's largest rum ball that weighed in at thirty-one kilos. Then came the best part—they got to eat it too.

INGREDIENTS:

- Chocolate and/or white cake crumbs—3 cups (504 g)
- Powdered sugar—¾ cup (146 g)
- Cocoa powder—¼ cup (34 g)
- Chopped pecans—1½ cups (180 g)
- Vanilla—1 teaspoon (5 mL)
- Corn syrup—3 Tablespoons (45 mL)
- Rum—½ cup (120 mL)

INSTRUCTIONS:

1. Add all ingredients to a mixing bowl and mix at second speed for 3 minutes until smooth.
2. Scoop and shape the dough into 1-inch balls or larger. Use about 4 teaspoons (20 mL) of the chocolate mixture per ball, which equals 2 level scoops from a small OXO cookie scoop.
3. Roll rum balls in additional confectioners' sugar, cocoa, sprinkles, nuts, or something else you like. Store in an airtight container in the refrigerator for several days to develop the flavor.

Yields about twenty 4 oz. (112 g) rum balls

Acknowledgements

As with all of our endeavors, this book has been a labor of love years in the making. And, as every baker knows, the best baked goods rely on using the best ingredients, and we have been blessed with an abundance on this project. We had the idea for this book while we were in the process of shooting our television series *It's a Sweet World*. We started down the path after our publicist Elizabeth Much arranged for an interview with journalist Debra Eckerling of the *Jewish Journal*. The article put momentum behind our effort, and we want to thank Elizabeth and Debra for getting the ball rolling. Likewise, our dear friend and big-time booster Steven Paul, chairman and CEO of Crystal Sky Pictures, not only encouraged us to pursue the idea but introduced us to literary agent extraordinaire Alan Nevins of Renaissance Literary Agency, who occupies his own vaunted place in Hollywood. He met with us the same day we gave him the proposal and then rolled up his sleeves, refashioned our book proposal, and spent months putting his time, energy, and experience into helping us turn our idea into a real book. We appreciate and are grateful for his guidance, belief, and unlimited positivity. The world needs more people with Alan's ability to create goodness. Thanks to him, we partnered with the hugely talented team at Mango Publishing led by publisher Brenda Knight, who took an initial Zoom meeting with us and said, "Let's make a great book." That same spirit was echoed by Mango's president and CEO Chris McKenney. We are indebted to both of you and the entire Mango staff of editors, sales and marketing people, data crunchers, and so on—they're just a terrific and smart group of people. Photographer Willie Sanjuan turned our food into art for this book, and we are thrilled that he added Bea's Bakery to his impressive resume, so many thanks to him. And the same for writer and collaborator Wendy Holden, who listened to our stories and put them most impressively on the pages of this book. More gratitude and lots of "Wow, we are so fortunate to work with these people." Our friends Shelli Azoff and Ziggy Gruber have been extremely supportive and helpful along the way. They dropped everything in their busy lives when we turned to them for feedback; that's friendship to be treasured and why we are honored they agreed to share their thoughts in the front of this book. Thank you.

On an even more personal note, Adaeze wants to thank and acknowledge with great heartfelt love David Jonathan Rogers Weber, who passed away in August 2024. He was a father figure and dear friend who knew of and encouraged Adaeze's vision for this book. He was instrumental in everything she pursued in her life since a chance meeting twenty-three years ago in New York. He always told her to reach for the stars and always believed in her, especially during those times when she needed to hear someone say, "You can do it!" Lenny wants to acknowledge the support of the Kardel family, family friends for more than four decades. And, above all else, Lenny wants to express his love and appreciation for his father, Robert Rosenberg. He took Lenny under his wing when he was seventeen years old, taught him the bakery business, and in the process gave him direction, meaning, and purpose. "I learned everything about baking from him," he says.

Finally, we want to send a nod of thanks heavenward to Jules Litwak for being a *mensch* when he sold Bea's to Lenny. We also want to thank Bea's Bakery itself—everyone who has ever worked there and everyone who has walked through the door looking for a nosh or a nibble, a little sweet or something more to take home. We take great pride in the tradition of Bea's and the new traditions we are creating. The bakery business is a people business, a smile business, and a hug business. Thank you to all who make it possible for us to share the magic of Bea's Bakery.

About the Authors

Lenny Rosenberg was born and raised in Plainview, Long Island. Since the tender age of seven, he was immersed in the family business of bakeries and cafes from the East to the West Coast. His father, Robert Rosenberg, was a seasoned pro at rebranding bakery establishments for over fifty years, including the landmark Éclairs in New York City. Lenny worked steadily in the family businesses until eventually the torch was passed to him. He bought and rebranded his first bakery at the age of seventeen.

Success quickly ensued, and Lenny continued to purchase and rebrand multiple bakeries and cafes. In 2000, he searched for a new challenge by moving out west, where he continued to rebrand great locations, one after another. It was in LA where Lenny met interior designer Adaeze Nwanonyiri. The duo decided that, at every location Lenny would buy and rebrand, Adaeze would put her designing skills to work. Lenny and Adaeze have rebranded such notable California bakeries and cafes as Nosh of Beverly Hills, 17th Street Café, Marmalade Café & Bakery on Montana Ave., Junior's bakery in Westwood, and, of course, the beloved Bea's Bakery in Los Angeles.

. . .

The best in her field was born in Houston, Texas, and pursued interior decorating studies at New York School of Interior Design. To pay her rent and school fees, she would consult and design her friends' apartments from basic "blah" to fabulous sanctuaries. Soon word of mouth grew, and she began to help local restaurants display an aesthetic vision to match their food and locations. Adaeze was called "the Expert Interior Decorator."

After a seven-year relationship with New York, Adaeze yearned for new challenges and a change of scenery and moved to Los Angeles, California, in the year 2000. One night, while attending a PR event in Malibu, California, she crossed paths with Lenny Rosenberg, the bakery and restaurant owner extraordinaire. The two hit it off, and Adaeze decided to put her interior design skills to work in every one of Lenny's locations. Now, they take the country by storm with their unbeatable track record with rebranding and bakeries and restaurants. Soon after they were well known for both their accomplishments and being husband and wife!

Mango Publishing, established in 2014, publishes an eclectic list of books by diverse authors—both new and established voices—on topics ranging from business, personal growth, women's empowerment, LGBTQ studies, health, and spirituality to history, popular culture, time management, decluttering, lifestyle, mental wellness, aging, and sustainable living. We were named 2019 *and* 2020's #1 fastest growing independent publisher by *Publishers Weekly*. Our success is driven by our main goal, which is to publish high-quality books that will entertain readers as well as make a positive difference in their lives.

Our readers are our most important resource; we value your input, suggestions, and ideas. We'd love to hear from you—after all, we are publishing books for you!

Please stay in touch with us and follow us at:

    Facebook: Mango Publishing
    Twitter: @MangoPublishing
    Instagram: @MangoPublishing
    LinkedIn: Mango Publishing
    Pinterest: Mango Publishing
    Newsletter: mangopublishinggroup.com/newsletter

Join us on Mango's journey to reinvent publishing, one book at a time.